THE HONEY GATHERERS

Books by Maura Dooley

POETRY COLLECTIONS

Ivy Leaves & Arrows (Bloodaxe Books, 1986)
Turbulence (Giant Steps, 1988)
Explaining Magnetism (Bloodaxe Books, 1991)
Kissing a Bone (Bloodaxe Books, 1996)
Sound Barrier: Poems 1982-2002 (Bloodaxe Books, 2002)

ANTHOLOGIES

Making for Planet Alice: New Women Poets (Bloodaxe Books, 1997)
How Novelists Work (Seren, 2000)
The Honey Gatherers: a book of love poems (Bloodaxe Books, 2003)

THE
Honey Gatherers

A BOOK OF LOVE POEMS

edited by
MAURA DOOLEY

BLOODAXE BOOKS

Selection and introduction copyright © 2003 Maura Dooley.

Copyright of poems rests with authors and other rights
holders as cited in the acknowledgements on pages 296–300,
which constitute an extension of this copyright page.

ISBN: 1 85224 359 7

First published 2003 by
Bloodaxe Books Ltd,
Highgreen,
Tarset,
Northumberland NE48 1RP.

www.bloodaxebooks.com
For further information about Bloodaxe titles
please visit our website or write to
the above address for a catalogue.

Bloodaxe Books Ltd acknowledges
the financial assistance of Northern Arts.

Cover printing by J. Thomson Colour Printers Ltd, Glasgow.

Printed in Great Britain by
Cromwell Press Ltd, Trowbridge, Wiltshire.

CONTENTS

6 'Wild Nights – Wild Nights!'

7 'How do I love thee?'

10 'I am no good at love'

11 'The end of love'

PREFACE

The Honey Gatherers takes its title from a phrase in Michael Ondaatje's 'The Cinnamon Peeler', a poem which describes the need to be marked, and marked out, by love. The choice of poems here reflects a desire to see together well-known, much-loved verse and little-known surprises. Each poem had to earn its place and detonate a charge, large or small, in the imagination and the memory. Each poem had to add something distinctive to our comprehension of the matter of love: something of the search, the sweetness, the sting and the death of love.

The field is enormous. I have had to make hard choices and leave out fine poems. Some of my choices have had to be between subtly different translations, or the many available versions of the same poem. In such cases I have always tried to imagine a new reader meeting the poem for the first time and asked myself which version I felt would speak most directly to them. I hope that the reader who is disappointed not to find some treasured old friend amongst these pages will instead make some interesting new acquaintances. Most of all, I hope that something of the delight I experienced in gathering work for this book rubs off on the reader.

I have grouped the poems in a way that allows for correspondences or illuminates differences, a way that suggests some of the various moods and moments of love. By this method I hope that each poem speaks in some way to the next and each group of poems builds a bridge in some way, to the next. There came a moment in the compilation, when the floor around me was covered over completely by poems. I had been arranging them as stepping-stones, by which to offer a reader safe passage through the book. Looking at that sea of paper I realised the idiocy in trying to order a safe passage through love. Love is not orderly.

Sometimes the placing side by side of two apparently similar poems only surprises and releases new truths about them. At other times, such a juxtaposition helps us notice more clearly the differences, rather than the superficial similarities. I hope the reader will find rigour as well as some tender surprises and wit in the final ordering of these poems. I would like to thank several friends who were kind enough to suggest particular poems, and Mary Enright and the staff of that treasure house, the Poetry Library, who were patient, efficient and helpful as ever.

One thing might be certain, whilst each of us understands what is meant by love in a unique way, each of us also looks for and recognises signs and expressions of it which confirm, amplify, translate or console our individual experiences. It is for this reason that the poetry of love will always be written and for this reason that the poetry of love will always be read.

MAURA DOOLEY

1

'What the heart is like'

(MIROSLAV HOLUB)

Love

Love is like a lamb, and love is like a lion;
Fly from love, he fights; fight, then does he fly on;
Love is all in fire, and yet is ever freezing;
Love is much in winning, yet is more in leezing;
Love is every sick, and yet is never dying;
Love is ever true, and yet is ever lying;
Love does dote in liking, and is mad in loathing;
Love indeed is anything, yet indeed is nothing.

THOMAS MIDDLETON (1580-1627)

What the heart is like

Officially the heart
is oblong, muscular,
and filled with longing.

But anyone who has painted the heart knows
that it is also

spiked like a star
and sometimes bedraggled
like a stray dog at night
and sometimes powerful
like an archangel's drum.

And sometimes cube-shaped
like a draughtsman's dream
and sometimes gaily round
like a ball in a net.

And sometimes like a thin line
and sometimes like an explosion.

And in it is
only a river,
a weir
and at most one little fish
by no means golden.

More like a grey
jealous
loach.

It certainly isn't noticeable
at first sight.

Anyone who has painted the heart knows
that first he had to
discard his spectacles,
his mirror,
throw away his fine-point pencil
and carbon paper

and for a long while
walk
outside.

MIROSLAV HOLUB (1923-98)
translated from the Czech by Ewald Osers

19

'So sweet love seemed that April morn'

So sweet love seemed that April morn,
When first we kissed beside the thorn,
So strangely sweet, it was not strange
We thought that love could never change.

But I can tell – let truth be told –
That love will change in growing old;
Though day by day is nought to see,
So delicate his motions be.

And in the end 'twill come to pass
Quite to forget what once he was,
Nor even in fancy to recall
The pleasure that was all in all.

His little spring, that sweet we found,
So deep in summer floods is drowned,
I wonder, bathed in joy complete,
How love so young could be so sweet.

ROBERT BRIDGES (1844-1930)

If Love Was Jazz

If love was jazz,
I'd be dazzled
By its razzmatazz.

If love was a sax
I'd melt in its brassy flame
Like wax.

If love was a guitar,
I'd pluck its six strings,
Eight to the bar.

If love was a trombone,
I'd feel its slow
Slide, right down my backbone.

If love was a drum,
I'd be caught in its snare,
Kept under its thumb.

If love was a trumpet,
I'd blow it.

If love was jazz,
I'd sing its praises,
Like Larkin has.

But love isn't jazz.
It's an organ recital.
Eminently worthy,
Not nearly as vital.

If love was jazz,
I'd always want more.
I'd be a regular
On that smoky dance-floor.

LINDA FRANCE (b. 1958)

Looking for Love

This woman looking for love
has to mend all the sails
that a winter of storms has ripped
to shreds, she will be sewing for years.

This guy must be looking for love.
See how he crouches like a runner
before the race.

Another man looking for love
crawls smiling up the phosphor mountains
of hell, the burning acrid slopes.

Two teenage girls speeding along
the towpath on golden-wheeled bikes,
are they looking for love?
Or are their shadows flying
over the naked Thames enough for them?

This woman looking for love
finds one tear in the rain.
If love were the remains
of a small wild horse,
or the skull of a young boy
lost in the wreck
of 'The Association',
she would have found love.

Two spitting cats
couple in the moonlit yard.
Is this love? thinks the peeping child.
She hopes not.

This woman looking for love
gets the door slammed in her face.
He's got too many wives already...

This fella looks for love
in the National Gallery,
he thinks he's Little Christ
snuggling and glittering on a Renaissance lap;
mother's boy,

whereas his wife,
rehearsing the Virtues and their Contraries,
finds love without looking,
in a room on the fourth floor of an ethereal hotel;
she doesn't ask his name.

PENELOPE SHUTTLE (*b.* 1947)

Just Once

Just once I knew what life was for.
In Boston, quite suddenly, I understood;
walked there along the Charles River,
watched the lights copying themselves,
all neoned and strobe-hearted, opening
their mouths as wide as opera singers;
counted the stars, my little campaigners,
my scar daisies, and knew that I walked my love
on the night green side of it and cried
my heart to the eastbound cars and cried
my heart to the westbound cars and took
my truth across a small humped bridge
and hurried my truth, the charm of it, home
and hoarded these constants into morning
only to find them gone.

ANNE SEXTON (1928-74)

Flowers

Some men never think of it.
You did. You'd come along
And say you'd nearly brought me flowers
But something had gone wrong.

The shop was closed. Or you had doubts –
The sort that minds like ours
Dream up incessantly. You thought
I might not want your flowers.

It made me smile and hug you then.
Now I can only smile.
But, look, the flowers you nearly brought
Have lasted all this while.

WENDY COPE (*b.* 1945)

23

Family album

No one in this family has ever died of love.
No food for myth and nothing magisterial.
Consumptive Romeos? Juliets diptherial?
A doddering second childhood was enough.
No death-defying vigils, love-struck poses
over unrequited letters strewn with tears!
Here, in conclusion, as scheduled, appears
a portly, pince-nez'd neighbor bearing roses.
No suffocation-in-the-closet gaffes
because the cuckold returned home too early!
Those frills or furbelows, however flounced and whirly,
barred no one from the family photographs.
No Bosch-like hell within their souls, no wretches
found bleeding in the garden, shirts in stains!
(True, some did die with bullets in their brains,
for other reasons, though, and on field stretchers.)
Even this belle with rapturous coiffure
who may have danced till dawn – but nothing smarter –
hemorrhaged to a better world, *bien sûr*,
but not to taunt or hurt *you*, slick-haired partner.
For others, Death was mad and monumental –
not for these citizens of a sepia past.
Their griefs turned into smiles, their days flew fast,
their vanishing was due to influenza.

WISLAWA SZYMBORSKA (b. 1923)
translated from the Polish by
Stanislaw Baranczak & Clare Cavanagh

2

'What is to be given'

(DELMORE SCHWARTZ)

In Paris with You

Don't talk to me of love. I've had an earful
And I get tearful when I've downed a drink or two.
I'm one of your talking wounded.
I'm a hostage. I'm maroonded.
But I'm in Paris with you.

Yes I'm angry at the way I've been bamboozled
And resentful at the mess that I've been through.
I admit I'm on the rebound
And I don't care where are *we* bound.
I'm in Paris with you.

    Do you mind if we do *not* go to the Louvre,
    If we say sod off to sodding Notre Dame,
    If we skip the Champs Elysées
    And remain here in this sleazy
    Old hotel room
    Doing this and that
    To what and whom
    Learning who you are,
    Learning what I am.

Don't talk to me of love. Let's talk of Paris,
The little bit of Paris in our view.
There's that crack across the ceiling
And the hotel walls are peeling
And I'm in Paris with you.

Don't talk to me of love. Let's talk of Paris.
I'm in Paris with the slightest thing you do.
I'm in Paris with your eyes, your mouth,
I'm in Paris with... all points south.
Am I embarrassing you?
I'm in Paris with you.

JAMES FENTON (*b.* 1949)

A Drinking Song

Wine comes in at the mouth
And love comes in at the eye;
That's all we shall know for truth
Before we grow old and die.
I lift the glass to my mouth,
I look at you, and I sigh.

W.B. YEATS (1865-1939)

'She was a Phantom of delight'

She was a Phantom of delight
When first she gleam'd upon my sight;
A lovely Apparition, sent
To be a moment's ornament;
Her eyes as stars of Twilight fair;
Like Twilight's too, her dusky hair;
But all things else about her drawn
From May-time and the cheerful Dawn;
A dancing Shape, an Image gay,
To haunt, to startle, and way-lay.

I saw her upon nearer view,
A Spirit, yet a Woman too!
Her household motions light and free,
And steps of virgin-liberty;
A countenance in which did meet
Sweet records, promises as sweet;
A Creature not too bright or good
For human nature's daily food;
For transient sorrows, simple wiles,
Praise, blame, love, kisses, tears, and smiles.

And now I see with eye serene
The very pulse of the machine;
A Being breathing thoughtful breath,
A Traveller between life and death;
The reason firm, the temperate will,
Endurance, foresight, strength, and skill;
A perfect Woman, nobly planned,
To warn, to comfort and command;
And yet a Spirit still, and bright
With something of angelic light.

WILLIAM WORDSWORTH (1770-1850)

Juliet

How did the party go in Portman Square?
I cannot tell you; Juliet was not there.
And how did lady Gaster's party go?
Juliet was next me and I do not know.

HILAIRE BELLOC (1870-1953)

When Molly Smiles

When Molly smiles beneath her cow,
I feel my heart – I can't tell how;
When Molly is on Sunday dressed,
On Sundays I can take no rest.

What can I do? On working days
I leave my work on her to gaze.
What shall I say? At sermons, I
Forget the text when Molly's by.

Good master curate, teach me how
To mind your preaching and my plough:
And if for this you'll raise a spell,
A good fat goose shall thank you well.

ANONYMOUS

My Little Lize

Who is de prutties' gal you say?
Oh, hush up man an go away.
Yo don't know w'at yo talkin bout;
Yo ought to go an fin' dat out.
De prutties' gal dat one can meet
Dat ever walk along de street;
I guess yo never seen my Lize;
If yo had seen her – bless yo eyes,
Yo would be sure to 'gree wid me,
Dat she's de sweetes' gal dat be.
Why man! Where was yo all dis time,
Dat yo don't see dis gal of mine?
Her skin is black an smoode as silk;
Her teet' is jus' as white as milk;
Her hair is of dem fluffy kin',
Wid curls a-hangin, black an shine.
Her shape is such dat can't be beat;
So graceful, slender an so neat.
W'ene'er she turn her eyes on you,
Dey seem to strike yo t'rough an t'rough,
Dere's not a sweeter lookin face;
An lips dat mek yo feel to tas'e.

Her hands is small an so's her feet,
Wid such a pair of ankles neat!
W'en she goes out to tek a walk
She sets de people all to talk.
De gals dey envy her wid fear,
Dey feel so cheap w'en she is near.
De boys dey lif' dere hats an try
To win a smile as she pass by.
But w'at's de use o talkin' so;
An try such beauty here to show!
Yo better see wid yo own eyes
Dis sweet an lovely little Lize;
For if I try de evening t'rough,
I couldn't quite explain to you.

JAMES S. MARTINEZ (*c*.1860–*c*.1945)

Meeting Point

Time was away and somewhere else,
There were two glasses and two chairs
And two people with the one pulse
(Somebody stopped the moving stairs):
Time was away and somewhere else.

And they were neither up nor down,
The stream's music did not stop
Flowing through heather, limpid brown,
Although they sat in a coffee shop
And they were neither up nor down.

The bell was silent in the air
Holding its inverted poise –
Between the clang and clang a flower,
A brazen calyx of no noise:
The bell was silent in the air.

The camels crossed the miles of sand
That stretched around the cups and plates;
The desert was their own, they planned
To portion out the stars and dates:
The camels crossed the miles of sand.

Time was away and somewhere else.
The waiter did not come, the clock
Forgot them and the radio waltz
Came out like water from a rock:
Time was away and somewhere else.

Her fingers flicked away the ash
That bloomed again in tropic trees:
Not caring if the markets crash
When they had forests such as these,
Her fingers flicked away the ash.

God or whatever means the Good
Be praised that time can stop like this,
That what the heart has understood
Can verify in the body's peace
God or whatever means the Good.

Time was away and she was here
And life no longer what it was,
The bell was silent in the air
And all the room a glow because
Time was away and she was here.

LOUIS MACNEICE (1907-63)

Song

Honest lover whatsoever,
If in all thy love there ever
Was one wav'ring thought, if thy flame
Were not still even still the same:
       Know this,
     Thou lov'st amiss,
     And to love true,
Thou must begin again, and love anew.

If when she appears i' th' room,
Thou dost not quake, and are struck dumb,
And in striving this to cover,
Dost not speak thy words twice over,
       Know this,
     Thou lov'st amiss,
     And to love true,
Thou must begin again, and love anew.

If fondly thou dost not mistake,
And all defects for graces take,
Persuad'st thyself that jests are broken,
When she hath little or nothing spoken,
       Know this,
     Thou lov'st amiss,
     And to love true,
Thou must begin again, and love anew.

If when thou appearest to be within,
Thou lett'st not men ask and ask again;
And when thou answerest, if it be,
To what was ask'd thee, properly,
       Know this,
     Thou lov'st amiss,
     And to love true,
Thou must begin again, and love anew.

If when thy stomach calls to eat,
Thou cutt'st not fingers 'stead of meat,
And with much gazing on her face
Dost not rise hungry from the place,

Know this,
Thou lov'st amiss,
And to love true,
Thou must begin again, and love anew.

If by this thou dost discover
That thou art no perfect lover,
And desiring to love true,
Thou dost begin to love anew:
Know this,
Thou lov'st amiss,
And to love true,
Thou must begin again, and love anew.

SIR JOHN SUCKLING (1609-42)

'It seems to me that man is equal to the gods'

It seems to me that man is equal to the gods,
that is, whoever sits opposite you
and, drawing nearer, savours, as you speak,
the sweetness of your voice

and the thrill of your laugh, which have so stirred the heart
in my own breast, that whenever I catch
sight of you, even if for a moment,
then my voice deserts me

and my tongue is struck silent, a delicate fire
suddenly races underneath my skin,
my eyes see nothing, my ears whistle like
the whirling of a top

and sweat pours down me and a trembling creeps over
my whole body, I am greener than grass;
at such times, I seem to be no more than
a step away from death;

but all can be endured since even a pauper...

SAPPHO (7th century BC)
translated from the Greek by Josephine Balmer

Faintheart in a Railway Train

At nine in the morning there passed a church,
At ten there passed me by the sea,
At twelve a town of smoke and smirch,
At two a forest of oak and birch,
    And then, on a platform, she:

A radiant stranger, who saw not me.
I said, 'Get out to her do I dare?'
But I kept my seat in my search for a plea,
And the wheels moved on. O could it but be
    That I had alighted there!

THOMAS HARDY (1848-1928)

The Subway

The subway flatters like the dope habit,
For a nickel extending peculiar space:
You dive from the street, holing like a rabbit,
Roar up a sewer with a millionaire's face.

Squatting in the full glare of the locked express
Imprisoned, rocked, like a man by a friend's death,
O how the immense investment soothes distress,
Credit laps you like a huge religious myth.

It's a sound effect. The trouble is seeing
(So anaesthetised) a square of bare throat
Or the fold at the crotch of a clothed human being:
You'll want to nuzzle it, crop at it like a goat.

That's not in the buy. The company between stops
Offers you security, and free rides to cops.

EDWIN DENBY (1903-83)

Coffee Shop

Most evenings
he comes in
about this time.

Espresso,
cigarette,
an intelligent paper.

A seat
by the window,
facing in.

Jeans, jumper
and black brogues.
I like those.

I wipe the table,
sometimes twice.
When I lean over

with his cup
my apron tightens,
just a touch.

Most evenings
he comes in
about this time.

I always think
he won't.
And then he does.

VICTOR TAPNER (*b.* 1950)

What Is To Be Given

What is to be given,
Is spirit, yet animal,
Colored, like heaven,
Blue, yellow, beautiful.

The blood is checkered by
So many stains and wishes,
Between it and the sky
You could not choose, for riches.

Yet let me now be careful
Not to give too much
To one so shy and fearful
For like a gun is touch.

DELMORE SCHWARTZ (1913-66)

The Leaves' Audible Smile

The leaves' audible smile
is no more than the breeze over there.
If I look at you and you look at me,
who is the first one to smile?
The first to smile laughs.

Laughs, and looks suddenly,
with the idea of not looking,
at where they sense in the leaves
the sound of the wind passing.
All is wind and dissembling.

But that look, from looking
where it does not look, turned;
and the two of us are talking
of what was unspoken.
Is this ending or begun?

FERNANDO PESSOA (1888-1935)
translated from the Portuguese by Paul Hyland

Song

Love and harmony combine,
And around our souls entwine,
While thy branches mix with mine,
And our roots together join.

Joys upon our branches sit,
Chirping loud, and singing sweet;
Like gentle streams beneath our feet
Innocence and virtue meet.

Thou the golden fruit dost bear,
I am clad in flowers fair;
Thy sweet boughs perfume the air,
And the turtle buildeth there.

There she sits and feeds her young,
Sweet I hear her mournful song;
And thy lovely leaves among,
There is Love: I hear his tongue.

There his charming nest doth lay,
There he sleeps the night away;
There he sports along the day,
And doth among our branches play.

WILLIAM BLAKE (1757-1827)

The Loser

> *A man thinks of the woman he once loved: first,*
> *after her wedding, and then nearly a decade later.*

1

I kissed you, bride and lost, and went
home from that bourgeois sacrament,
your cheek still tasting cold upon

37

my lips that gave you benison
with all the swagger that they knew –
as losers somehow learn to do.

Your wedding made my eyes ache; soon
the world would be worse off for one
more golden apple dropped to ground
without the least protesting sound,
and you would windfall lie, and we
forget your shimmer on the tree.

Beauty is always wasted: if
not Mignon's song sung to the deaf,
at all events to the unmoved.
A face like yours cannot be loved
long or seriously enough.
Almost, we seem to hold it off.

    2

Well, you are tougher than I thought.
Now when the wash with ice hangs taut
this morning of St Valentine,
I see you strip the squeaking line,
your body weighed against the load,
and all my groans can do no good.

Because you still are beautiful,
though squared and stiffened by the pull
of what nine windy years have done.
You have three daughters, lost a son.
I see all your intelligence
flung into that unwearied stance.

My envy is of no avail.
I turn my head and wish him well
who chafed your beauty into use
and lives forever in a house
lit by the friction of your mind.
You stagger in against the wind.

ADRIENNE RICH (*b.* 1929)

The Planter's Daughter

When night stirred at sea
And the fire brought a crowd in,
They say that her beauty
Was music in mouth
And few in the candlelight
Thought her too proud,
For the house of the planter
Is known by the trees.

Men that had seen her
Drank deep and were silent,
The women were speaking
Wherever she went –
As a bell that is rung
Or a wonder told shyly,
And O she was the Sunday
In every week.

AUSTIN CLARKE (1896-1974)

On Raglan Road
(AIR: *The Dawning of the Day*)

On Raglan Road on an autumn day I met her first and knew
That her dark hair would weave a snare that I might one day rue;
I saw the danger, yet I walked along the enchanted way,
And I said, let grief be a fallen leaf at the dawning of the day.

On Grafton Street in November we tripped lightly along the ledge
Of the deep ravine where can be seen the worth of passion's pledge,
The Queen of Hearts still making tarts and I not making hay –
O I loved too much and by such by such is happiness thrown away.

I gave her gifts of the mind I gave her the secret sign that's known
To the artists who have known the true gods of sound and stone
And word and tint. I did not stint for I gave her poems to say.
With her own name there and her own dark hair like clouds over
      fields of May.

On a quiet street where old ghosts meet I see her walking now
Away from me so hurriedly my reason must allow
That I had wooed not as I should a creature made of clay –
When the angel wooes the clay he'd lose his wings at the dawn of day.

PATRICK KAVANAGH (1905-67)

The Water Bearer

When I walk in the streets at night
Following the lamplight to where it falls
Exhausted in my head, some girl
Still carries my love on her shoulders through the crowd
Which sometimes offers up her face to me
Like a book which flickers shut again.

So long I have tried to touch that face
When it drifts for a moment near me on the tide
So many times
I have seen it sucked back into the sea
Of all such nights I follow down like stones
To where they lie unfound, unfathomable.

When I wake in the morning, far from her,
This girl, wherever she is sleeping, wakes with me
And takes up the weight of my love for her.
Carrying it back into the world of absences
Where I see her walking alone in the streets
Cursed as she is with being mine.

For her shoulders that are always disappearing
Into the heart of her own searching
Look so calm and beautiful despite it all
That I wait impatiently for the sight of her
Passing again so sweetly through my life
As if she carried water from a well.

HUGO WILLIAMS (*b.* 1942)

Gifts

'I will bring you love,' said the young lover,
'A glad light to dance in your dark eye.
Pendants I will bring of the white bone,
And gay parrot feathers to deck your hair.'
But she only shook her head.

'I will put a child in you arms,' he said,
'Will be a great headman, great rain-maker.
I will make remembered songs about you
That all the tribes in all the wandering camps
Will sing for ever.'

But she was not impressed,

'I will bring you the still moonlight on the lagoon,
And steal for you the singing of all the birds;
I will bring down the stars of heaven to you,
And put the bright rainbow into your hand.'

'No, she said, 'bring me tree-grubs.'

OODGEROO of the tribe Noonuccal (*b.* 1920)

A Blade of Grass

You ask for a poem.
I offer you a blade of grass.
You say it is not good enough.
You ask for a poem.

I say this blade of grass will do.
It has dressed itself in frost,
It is more immediate
Than any image of my making.

You say it is not a poem,
It is a blade of grass and grass
Is not quite good enough.
I offer you a blade of grass.

41

You are indignant.
You say it is too easy to offer grass.
It is absurd.
Anyone can offer a blade of grass.

You ask for a poem.
And so I write you a tragedy about
How a blade of grass
Becomes more and more difficult to offer,

And about how as you grow older
A blade of grass
Becomes more difficult to accept.

BRIAN PATTEN (*b.* 1946)

I Wouldn't Thank You for a Valentine
(rap)

I wouldn't thank you for a Valentine.
I won't wake up early wondering if the postman's been.
Should 10 red-padded satin hearts arrive with sticky sickly saccharine
Sentiments in very vulgar verses I wouldn't wonder if you meant them.
Two dozen anonymous Interflora roses?
I'd not bother to swither over who sent them!
I wouldn't thank you for a Valentine.

Scrawl SWALK across the envelope
I'd just say 'Same Auld Story
I canny be bothered deciphering it –
I'm up to here with Amore!
The whole Valentine's Day Thing is trivial and commercial,
A cue for unleasing clichés and candyheart motifs to which I personally
      am not partial.'
Take more than singing Telegrams, or pints of Chanel Five or sweets –
To get me ordering oysters or ironing my black satin sheets.
I wouldn't thank you for a Valentine.

If you sent me a solitaire and promises solemn,
Took out an ad in the *Guardian* Personal Column
Saying something very soppy such as 'Who Loves Ya, Poo?

I'll tell you, I do, Fozzy Bear, that's who!'
You'd entirely fail to charm me, in fact I'd detest it
I wouldn't be eighteen again for anything, I'm glad I'm past it.
I wouldn't thank you for a Valentine.

If you sent me a single orchid, or a pair of Janet Reger's in a
       heart-shaped box and declared your Love Eternal
I'd say I'd not be caught dead in them they were politically suspect
       and I'd rather something thermal.
If you hired a plane and blazed our love in a banner across the skies;
If you bought me something flimsy in a flatteringly wrong size;
If you sent me a postcard with three Xs and told me how you felt
I wouldn't thank you, I'd melt.

LIZ LOCHHEAD (*b.* 1947)

'The Way I read a Letter'

The Way I read a Letter's – this –
'Tis first – I lock the door –
And push it with my fingers – next –
For transport it be sure –

And then I go the furthest off
To counteract a knock –
Then draw my little Letter forth
And slowly pick the lock –

Then – glancing narrow, at the Wall –
And narrow at the floor
For firm Conviction of a Mouse
Not exorcised before –

Peruse how infinite I am
To no one that You – know –
And sigh for lack of Heaven – but not
The Heaven God bestow –

EMILY DICKINSON (1830-86)

The Poet speaks to the loved one by telephone

Your voice watered the sandhill of my heart
in that sweet wooden cabin.
Spring blossomed to the south of my feet,
to the north, a flower of bracken.

A pine of light through the narrow space
sang without dawn, without a source,
while for the first time my grief
hung crowns of hope across the roof.

That sweet and distant voice poured through me.
That sweet and distant voice renewed me.
Sweet, distant, muffled tone.

Remote as a dark wounded doe.
And sweet as sobbing in the snow.
Sweet, distant, in my bone!

FEDERICO GARCÍA LORCA (1898-1936)
translated from the Spanish by Merryn Williams

The Telephone

'When I was just as far as I could walk
From here today,
There was an hour
All still
When leaning with my head against a flower
I heard you talk.
Don't say I didn't, for I heard you say –
You spoke from that flower on the windowsill –
Do you remember what it was you said?'

'First tell me what it was you thought you heard.'

'Having found the flower and driven a bee away,
I leaned my head,
And holding by the stalk,
I listened and I thought I caught the word –
What was it? Did you call me by my name?
Or did you say –
Someone said "Come" – I heard it as I bowed.'

'I may have thought as much, but not aloud.'

'Well, so I came.'

ROBERT FROST (1874-1963)

Lovesick

I'm scared of my own heart beat;
it's so loud someone might say
'who's on the drums?' and I'd blush
(not exactly beetroot) but blush
all the same.

I have these feelings.
I take them home from school
and tuck them up. In the morning
I say all the wrong things by accident
again and again.

Like, for instance, shouting *Miss*
in the middle of someone else saying
something. Usually Agnes MacNamara.
'In a minute,' says Miss. And I blush.
I hate MacNamara.

Miss is from Bangladesh and has
thick black hair, usually brushed
into one sleek pony. If I could tie the bow!
She has lovely eyes, dark pools.
Miss isn't married.

But I expect she will get married soon.
I think Mr Hudson wants to marry her.
Mr Hudson is always waiting in the corridor.
Him or that Agnes MacNamara.
Will I ever. Will I ever

Get older so that it doesn't hurt.
So that my heart doesn't hurt.
So that I don't spend all my time
with my fingers crossed and wishing:
Say something nice. Miss, Please. *Something.*

JACKIE KAY (*b.* 1961)

Love: Beginnings

They're at that stage where so much desire streams between them,
      so much frank need and want,
so much absorption in the other and the self and the self-admiring
      entity and unity they make –
her mouth so full, breast so lifted, head thrown back *so* far in her
      laughter at his laughter,
he so solid, planted, oaky, firm, so resonantly factual in the headiness
      of being craved so,
she almost wreathed upon him as they intertwine again, touch again,
      cheek, lip, shoulder, brow,
every glance moving toward the sexual, every glance away soaring
      back in flame into the sexual –
that just to watch them is to feel again that hitching in the groin, that
      filling of the heart,
the old, sore heart, the battered, foundered, faithful heart, snorting
      again, stamping in its stall.

C.K. WILLIAMS (*b.* 1936)

Dewpond and Black Drain-pipes

In order to distract me, my mother
sent me on an Archaeology Week.
We lived in tents on the downs,
and walked over to the site
every morning. It was a Roman dewpond.

There was a boy there called Charlie.
He was the first boy I had really met.
I was too shy to go to the pub,
but I hung around the camp every night
waiting for him to come back.

He took no notice of me at first,
but one night the two of us
were on Washing-Up together.
I was dressed in a black jersey
and black drain-pipes, I remember.

You in mourning? he said.
He didn't know I was
one of the first beatniks.
He put a drying-up cloth
over my head and kissed me

through the linen BREEDS OF DOGS.
I love you, Charlie I said.
Later, my mother blamed herself
for what had happened. *The Romans
didn't even interest her*, she said.

SELIMA HILL (*b.* 1945)

Snow and Snow

Snow is sometimes a she, a soft one.
  Her kiss on your cheek, her finger on your sleeve
In early December, on a warm evening,
    And you turn to meet her, saying 'It's snowing!'
      But it is not. And nobody's there.
      Empty and calm is the air.

Sometimes the snow is a he, a sly one.
  Weakly he signs the dry stone with a damp spot.
Waifish he floats and touches the pond and is not.
    Treacherous-beggarly he falters, and taps at the window.
      A little longer he clings to the grass-blade tip
      Getting his grip.

Then how she leans, how furry foxwrap she nestles
  The sky with her warm, and the earth with her softness.
How her lit crowding fairytales sink through the space-silence
    To build her palace, till it twinkles in starlight –
      Too frail for a foot
      Or a crumb of soot.

Then how his muffled armies move in all night
  And we wake and every road is blockaded
Every hill taken and every farm occupied
    And the white glare of his tents is on the ceiling.
      And all that dull blue day and on into the gloaming
      We have to watch more coming.

Then everything in the rubbish-heaped world
  Is a bridesmaid at her miracle.
Dunghills and crumbly dark old barns are bowed in the chapel of
      her sparkle,
  The gruesome boggy cellars of the wood
    Are a wedding of lace
    Now taking place.

TED HUGHES (1930-98)

3

'What are all these kissings worth
If thou kiss not me?'

(SHELLEY)

Conviction IV

I like to get off with people,
I like to lie in their arms
I like to be held and lightly kissed,
Safe from all alarms.

I like to laugh and be happy
With a beautiful kiss,
I tell you, in all the world
There is no bliss like this.

STEVIE SMITH (1902-71)

The Kiss

'I saw you take his kiss!' ''Tis true.'
    'O, modesty!' ''Twas strictly kept:
He thought me asleep, at least I knew
    He thought I thought he thought I slept.'

COVENTRY PATMORE (1823-96)

The Look

Strephon kissed me in the spring,
    Robin in the fall,
But Colin only looked at me
    And never kissed at all.

Strephon's kiss was lost in jest,
    Robin's lost in play,
But the kiss in Colin's eyes
    Haunts me night and day.

SARA TEASDALE (1884-1933)

Love's Philosophy

The fountains mingle with the river,
   And the rivers with the ocean,
The winds of heaven mix for ever
   With a sweet emotion;
Nothing in the world is single;
   All things by a law divine
In one another's being mingle –
   Why not I with thine?

See the mountains kiss high heaven,
   And the waves clasp one another;
No sister flower would be forgiven
   If it disdained its brother:
And the sunlight clasps the earth,
   And the moonbeams kiss the sea,
What are all these kissings worth,
   If thou kiss not me?

PERCY BYSSHE SHELLEY (1792-1822)

In the Country

In the country there are youths
With the sweet breath of sucky calves
And their soft mouths.

ANNE HAVERTY (*b.* 1959)

A Love-Song

Such a heart!
Should he leave, how I'd miss him.
Jewel, acorn, youth.
Kiss him!

ANONYMOUS
translated from the Irish by Brendan Kennelly

Being Late to Meet You at the Station

That God-is-Light smile of your arms
One second before
I'm in them.

Your eyes, having nearly
Given up, lit up
As mythical

As Regent Street. A satyr
Reeling at the discovery of honey.
Your mouth,

Tasting of the breath
Of greenhouses. The sap.
The open stamens. Chlorophyll.

RUTH PADEL (*b.* 1947)

Jenny Kissed Me

Jenny kiss'd me when we met,
Jumping from the chair she sat in;
Time, you thief, who love to get
Sweets into your list, put that in!
Say I'm weary, say I'm sad,
Say that health and wealth have miss'd me,
Say I'm growing old, but add,
Jenny kiss'd me.

LEIGH HUNT (1784-1859)

'Time to live and let love, Lesbia'

Time to live and let love, Lesbia,
Count old men's cant and carping chatter
Cheap talk, not worth a penny piece.
You see, each sun can set, can rise again,
But when our brief light begins to wane,
Night brings one unending sleep.
So let me have a thousand kisses,
Then a hundred, then a thousand *gratis*,
A hundred, hundred thousand on increase.
Then, when we've made our first million,
We'll cook the books, just smear the sums,
In case some evil eye might spy or sully
By reckoning up our final tally.

CATULLUS (*c*.84-*c*.54 BC)
translated from the Latin by Josephine Balmer

Old Love and New

My love comes behind me
And he kisses me just where –
What has come in your minds now?
– Between neck and jersey
My bent neck is bare –
Are you thinking, are you thinking
That you might have been kinder?
– And I know that my hair
Curls a little, curls a little –
And your hands that remind me,
And your breath in my hair

My love comes behind me
And his lips are like bees –
What has come in my mind now?
– That light on the clover,
That settle and tease –
I am thinking, I am thinking,
As my eyes look out blindly
And I stiffen at the knees,
Of my new love, of my new love,
Who is fonder and kinder
And is far overseas.

NAOMI MITCHISON (1897-1997)

Bite

Dark corsage I can't
unpin, I'm stuck with it,
drawing wry comment
for days, however I hide
this stamp that approves

the boundary, proves that you
stop short of blood, all jokes
aside. But note
how readily my veins
leap up: a little harder and
the whole heart would follow,
I'd turn inside out, bleak pocket
for your rummaging,
magician's hat. And yet
I don't; I let you pass
like this small stormcloud on
my white, impassive throat.

TRACY RYAN (*b.* 1964)

The Frog Prince

I am a frog
I live under a spell
I live at the bottom
Of a green well

And here I must wait
Until a maiden places me
On her royal pillow
And kisses me
In her father's palace.

The story is familiar
Everybody knows it well
But do other enchanted people feel as nervous
As I do? The stories do not tell,

Ask if they will be happier
When the changes come
As already they are fairly happy
In a frog's doom?

I have been a frog now
For a hundred years
And in all this time
I have not shed many tears,

I am happy, I like the life,
Can swim for many a mile
(When I have hopped to the river)
And am for ever agile.

And the quietness,
Yes, I like to be quiet
I am habituated
To a quiet life,

But always when I think these thoughts
As I sit in my well
Another thought comes to me and says:
It is part of the spell

To be happy
To work up contentment
To make much of being a frog
To fear disenchantment

Says, It will be *heavenly*
To be set free,
Cries, *Heavenly* the girl who disenchants
And the royal times, *heavenly*,
And I think it will be.

Come then, royal girl and royal times,
Come quickly,
I can be happy until you come
But I cannot be heavenly,
Only disenchanted people
Can be heavenly.

STEVIE SMITH (1902-71)

'Dove-Love'

The dove purrs – over and over the dove
purrs its declaration. The wind's tone
changes from tree to tree, the creek on stone
alters its sob and fall, but still the dove
goes insistently on, telling its love
          'I could eat you.'

And in captivity, they say, doves do.
Gentle, methodical, starting with the feet
(the ham-pink succulent toes
on their thin stems of rose),
baring feather by feather the wincing meat:
          'I could eat you.'

That neat suburban head, that suit of grey,
watchful conventional eye and manicured claw –
these also rhyme with us. The doves play
on one repetitive note that plucks the raw
helpless nerve, their soft 'I do. I do.
          I could eat you.'

JUDITH WRIGHT (1915-2000)

The Amorous Cannibal

Suppose I were to eat you
I should probably begin
with the fingers, the cheeks and the breasts
yet all of you would tempt me,
so powerfully spicy
as to discompose my choice.

While I gobbled you up
delicacy by tidbit
I should lay the little bones
ever so gently round my late
and caress the bigger bones
like ivory talismans.

When I had quite devoured the edible you
(your tongue informing my voice-box)
I would wake in the groin of night
to feel, ever so slowly,
your plangent, ravishing ghost
munching my fingers and toes.

Here,
     with and awkward, delicate gesture
someone slides out his heart
and offers it on a spoon,
garnished with adjectives.

CHRIS WALLACE-CRABBE (*b.* 1934)

Muse

When I kiss you in all the folding places
of your body, you make that noise like a dog
dreaming, dreaming of the long runs he makes
in answer to some jolt to his hormones,
running across landfills, running, running
by tips and shorelines from the scent of too much,
but still going with head up and snout
in the air because he loves it all
and has to get away. I have to kiss deeper
and more slowly – your neck, your inner arm,
the neat creases under your toes, the shadow
behind your knee, the white angles of your groin –
until you fall quiet because only then
can I get the damned words to come into my mouth.

JO SHAPCOTT (*b.* 1953)

4

*'Let lovers go fresh and sweet
to be undone'*

(RICHARD WILBUR)

Night Shift

Once again I have missed you by moments;
steam hugs the rim of the just-boiled kettle,

water in the pipes finds its own level.
In another room there are other signs

of someone having left: dust, unsettled
by the sweep of the curtains; the clockwork

contractions of the paraffin heater.
For weeks now we have come and gone, woken

in acres of empty bedding, written
lipstick love-notes on the bathroom mirror

and in this space we have worked and paid for
we have found ourselves, but lost each other.

Upstairs, at least, there is understanding
in things more telling than lipstick kisses:

the air, still hung with spores of your hairspray;
body-heat stowed in the crumpled duvet.

SIMON ARMITAGE (*b.* 1963)

At the Wrong Door

A bank-manager's rapid signature
of hair on the bath enamel, twist
and tail, to confirm that I have missed
you by a minute; mat on the floor,

stamped vigorously with wet; your
absence palpable in the misty,
trickling, inexorcisable ghost
that occupies the whole mirror –

I cannot rub it away – the room
clings to me with such a perfume
of soap and sweat, that I can only

stop to think how somewhere else
you may be standing, naked, lonely,
amid a downfall of dampish towels.

CHRISTOPHER REID (*b.* 1949)

Steam

Not long ago so far, a lover and I
in a room of steam –

a sly, thirsty silvery word – lay down,
opposite ends, and vanished.

Quite recently, if one of us sat up,
or stood, or stretched, naked,

a nude pose in soft pencil
behind tissue paper

appeared, rubbed itself out, slow,
with a smokey cloth.

Say a matter of months. This hand reaching
through the steam

to touch the real thing, shockingly there,
not a ghost at all.

CAROL ANN DUFFY (*b.* 1955)

Gloire de Dijon

When she rises in the morning
I linger to watch her;
She spreads the bath-cloth underneath the window
And the sunbeams catch her
Glistening white on the shoulders,
While down her sides the mellow
Golden shadow glows as
She stoops to the sponge, and her swung breasts
Sway like full-blown yellow
Gloire de Dijon roses.

She drips herself with water, and her shoulders
Glisten as silver, they crumple up
Like wet and falling roses, and I listen
For the sluicing of their rain-dishevelled petals.
In the window full of sunlight
Concentrates her golden shadow
Fold on fold, until it glows as
Mellow as the glory roses.

D.H. LAWRENCE (1885-1930)

Love in a Bathtub

Years later we'll remember the bathtub,
the position
          of the taps
the water, slippery
as if a bucketful
          of eels had joined us...
we'll be old, our children grown up
but we'll remember the water
                    sloshing out
the useless soap,

62

the mountain of wet towels.
'Remember the bathtub in Belfast?'
we'll prod each other –

SUJATA BHATT (*b*. 1956)

Like the Touch of Rain

Like the touch of rain she was
On a man's flesh and hair and eyes
When the joy of walking thus
Has taken him by surprise:

With the love of the storm he burns,
He sings, he laughs, well I know how,
But forgets when he returns
As I shall not forget her 'Go now'.

Those two words shut a door
Between me and the blessed rain
That was never shut before
And will not open again.

EDWARD THOMAS (1878-1917)

All Legendary Obstacles

All legendary obstacles lay between
Us, the long imaginary plain,
The monstrous ruck of mountains
And, swinging across the night,
Flooding the Sacramento, San Joaquin,
The hissing drift of winter rain.

All day I waited, shifting
Nervously from station to bar
As I saw another train sail
By, the San Francisco Chief or
Golden Gate, water dripping
From great flanged wheels.

At midnight you came, pale
Above the negro porter's lamp.
I was too blind with rain
And doubt to speak, but
Reached from the platform
Until our chilled hands met.

You had been travelling for days
With an old lady, who marked
A neat circle on the glass
With her glove, to watch us
Move into the wet darkness
Kissing, still unable to speak.

JOHN MONTAGUE (*b.* 1929)

Love Calls Us to the Things of This World

    The eyes open to a cry of pulleys,
And spirited from sleep, the astounded soul
Hangs for a moment bodiless and simple
As false dawn.
               Outside the open window
The morning air is all awash with angels.

Some are in bed-sheets, some are in blouses,
Some are in smocks: but truly there they are.
Now they are rising together in calm swells
Of halcyon feeling, filling whatever they wear
With the deep joy of their impersonal breathing;

Now they are flying in place, conveying
The terrible speed of their omnipresence, moving
And staying like white water; and now of a sudden
They swoon down into so rapt a quiet
That nobody seems to be there.
                                        The soul shrinks

From all that it is about to remember,
From the punctual rape of every blessèd day,
And cries,
                'Oh, let there be nothing on earth but laundry,
Nothing but rosy hands in the rising steam
And clear dances done in the sight of heaven.'

Yet, as the sun acknowledges
With a warm look the world's hunks and colors,
The soul descends once more in bitter love
To accept the waking body, saying now
In a changed voice as the man yawns and rises,

'Bring them down from their ruddy gallows;
Let there be clean linen for the backs of thieves;
Let lovers go fresh and sweet to be undone,

And the heaviest nuns walk in a pure floating
Of dark habits,
                        keeping their difficult balance.'

RICHARD WILBUR (*b.* 1921)

Do

The winding-sheet
That is my life
May now be only
Half-undone.

Days that make
Ghosts of the living,
Turn the wedding-suit
Of the proud groom
Into the comical
Garb of a bent man
Shouldering a rake
In an August field.

Yet I still wait
To tell them
How when his key
Turns in the lock
The world
Enters the room.

And the winding-
Sheet that is my life
Winds tighter
Hour by hour.

ANNE HAVERTY (*b.* 1959)

Scarborough Fair

Can you make me a cambric shirt,
  Parsley, sage, rosemary, and thyme,
Without any seam or needlework?
  And you shall be a true lover of mine.

Can you wash it in yonder well,
  Parsley, sage, rosemary, and thyme,
Where never sprung water, nor rain ever fell?
  And you shall be a true lover of mine.

Can you dry it on yonder thorn,
  Parsley, sage, rosemary, and thyme,
Which never bore blossom since Adam was born?
  And you shall be a true lover of mine.

Now you've asked me questions three,
  Parsley, sage, rosemary, and thyme,
I hope you'll answer as many for me,
  And you shall be a true lover of mine.

Can you find me an acre of land,
  Parsley, sage, rosemary, and thyme,
Between the salt water and the sea sand?
  And you shall be a true lover of mine.

Can you plough it with a ram's horn,
  Parsley, sage, rosemary, and thyme,
And sow it all over with one peppercorn?
  And you shall be a true lover of mine.

Can you reap it with a sickle of leather,
  Parsley, sage, rosemary, and thyme,
And bind it up with a peacock's feather?
  And you shall be a true lover of mine.

When you have done and finished your work,
  Parsley, sage, rosemary, and thyme,
Then come to me for your cambric shirt,
  And you shall be a true lover of mine.

ANONYMOUS

The Shirt of a Lad

As I did the washing one day
Under the bridge at Aberteifi,
And a golden stick to drub it,
And my sweetheart's shirt beneath it –
A knight came by upon a charger,
Proud and swift and broad of shoulder,
And he asked if I would sell
The shirt of the lad that I loved well.

No, I said, I will not trade –
Not if a hundred pounds were paid;
Not if two hillsides I could keep
Full with wethers and white sheep;
Not if two fields full of oxen
Under yoke were in the bargain;
Not if the herbs of all Llanddewi,
Trodden and pressed, were offered to me –
Not for the likes of that, I'd sell
The shirt of the lad that I love well.

ANONYMOUS
translated from the Welsh by Tony Conran

His Shirt

does not show his
true colors. Ice-

blue and of stuff
so common

anyone
could have bought it,

his shirt
is known only

to me, and only
at certain times

of the day.
At dawn

it is a flag
in the middle

of a square
waiting to catch

chill light.
Unbuttoned, it's

a sail surprised
by boundless joy.

In candlelight at turns
a penitent's

scarf or beggar's
fleece, his shirt is

inapproachable.
It is the very shape

and tint
of desire

and could be mistaken
for something quite

fragile and
ordinary.

RITA DOVE (*b.* 1952)

Shirts

She hangs out his shirts,
pins them by the tails
to the singing line.

She hangs out his shirts,
and in the pure green
that the lawn paints them
she can see her face:
I am his wife.

In the attention
of cushions, the soft
elisions of a door –
a voice, her voice
comes back to her:
he is my husband,
I am his wife.

I am the place
he returns to, his
hunger's home.
I build every day
a houseful of rooms,
of walls to enfold
the things that he loves.

She hangs out his shirts,
and the air they breathe
fills them with flight:
his gentle arms rage
flailing at the sky,
scratching and clawing
to catch up with the wind.

She hangs out his shirts:
he is her husband,
she is his wife.

NIGEL JENKINS (*b.* 1949)

The Shirt of a Lad

Under the bridge at Ballyhoo
My love went down before the water,
My white shirt in her white hands.
A willow stick to whack it.

Who came by I did not see –
Wash away the weeping, wailing.
She brought it back to give to me
The cuffs behind her trailing.

Below the falls at Foofaraw
My love went down before the water,
My white shirt in her white hands.
A laurel stick to lam it.

Who rode by I could not hear –
Wash away the will, the wishing –
When she brought it back to me
A yard of tail was missing.

Beside the rocks at Rantan Bay
My love went down before the water,
My white shirt in her white hands.
A blackthorn stick to bat it.

Who came by I dare not name –
Wash away the fear to follow.
She brought it back to give to me
With brimstone on the collar.

Who rode by I know I know
Wash away the false, the failing –
Down the River Rowdydow
My once fine shirt goes sailing.

PETE MORGAN (*b.* 1939)

The Girl in the Calico Dress

In flowery July upon Healey's proud Height,
   As the plover sprung from the morass,
And southward the cuckoo was taking his flight,
   And the corncrake was deep in the grass;
The swallow and swift were aloft in the air,
   And the starling was feeding her young;
The milkmaid was tending her cattle with care,
   And the haymakers cheerfully sung –

     'The maidens of Burnley in satin or silk,
       Are pretty, I freely confess;
     But give me the maid who is neatly arrayed
       In a beautiful calico dress.'

They may praise the Italian ladies, in vain,
   Or the maidens of France or Peru,
Or worship the languishing beauties of Spain.
   And the blushing Circassians, too.
But she whom I love has an eye like the sloe,
   And her cheeks are like roses in June,
So graceful each step as she trips like the doe,
   And her sweet ruby lips are in tune.

     'The maidens of Burnley in satin or silk,
       Are pretty, I freely confess;
     But give me the maid who is neatly arrayed
       In a beautiful calico dress.'

Her dress (though of print) was embroidered with care,
   And the flowers on her bosom were sweet;
The zephyrs waved gently her dark curly hair,
   And the buttercups bloomed at her feet.
As dew from the daisies she carelessly dashed,
   The young men were all seized with surprise;
How sweetly she smiled, and what mischief she flashed
   From the glance of her dark rolling eyes.

'The maidens of Burnley in satin or silk,
　　Are pretty, I freely confess;
　But give me the maid who is neatly arrayed
　　In a beautiful calico dress.'

Should fortune or friendship impel me to roam,
　Or a thirst after changes constrain,
I'd still call the banks of Old Healey my home,
　And I'd sing of its beauties again.
Sweet gardens of roses, or art-cultured bowers,
　May delight a poor soul to possess;
But give me Old Healey, bedecked with wild flowers,
　And the girl in the calico dress.

'The maidens of Burnley in satin or silk,
　　Are pretty, I freely confess;
　But give me the maid who is neatly arrayed
　　In a beautiful calico dress.'

HENRY NUTTER (*d.* 1897)

The Linen Industry

Pulling up flax after the blue flowers have fallen
And laying our handfuls in the peaty water
To rot those grasses to the bone, or building stooks
That recall the skirts of an invisible dancer,

We become a part of the linen industry
And follow its processes to the grubby town
Where fields are compacted into window-boxes
And there is little room among the big machines.

But even in our attic under the skylight
We make love on a bleach green, the whole meadow
Draped with material turning white in the sun
As though snow reluctant to melt were our attire.

73

What's passion but a battering of stubborn stalks,
Then a gentle combing out of fibres like hair
And a weaving of these into christening robes,
Into garments for a marriage or funeral?

Since it's like a bereavement once the labour's done
To find ourselves last workers in a dying trade,
Let flax be our matchmaker, our undertaker,
The provider of sheets for whatever the bed –

And be shy of your breasts in the presence of death,
Say that you look more beautiful in linen
Wearing white petticoats, the bow on your bodice
A butterfly attending the embroidered flowers.

MICHAEL LONGLEY (*b*. 1939)

It was Summer, or the End of Summer

It was summer, or the end of summer
And I heard then your footsteps, as you went from east to west
For the last time. And in the world
Handkerchiefs were lost, and books, and people.

It was summer or the end of summer
There were hours in the afternoon,
You were;
And you wore your shroud
For the first time.
And you never noticed
Because it was embroidered with flowers.

YEHUDA AMICHAI (1924-2000)
translated from the Hebrew by Assia Gutman & Harold Schimmel
with the collaboration of Ted Hughes

5

'And our mouths run over with luscious smiles'

(DAVID CONSTANTINE)

It's Platonic

Platonic my eye,

I yearn
for the fullness
of your tongue
making me
burst forth
pleasure after pleasure
after dark,

soaking all my dreams.

RITA ANN HIGGINS (*b.* 1955)

Song: to Celia

Come, my Celia, let us prove
While we may, the sports of love.
Time will not be ours for ever:
He at length our good will sever.
Spend not then his gifts in vain.
Suns that set may rise again,
But if once we lose this light
'Tis with us perpetual night.
Why should we defer our joys?
Fame and rumour are but toys.
Cannot we delude the eyes
Of a few poor household spies?
Or his easier ears beguile
So removed by our wile?
'Tis no sin love's fruit to steal,
But the sweet theft to reveal –
To be taken, to be seen –
These have crimes accounted been.

BEN JONSON (1572-1637)

Get Down Ye Angels

Get down ye angels from the heights.
Try a few of earth's numinous delights:
the orgiastic rustling of the grass.
The wind's brazen feather tickling your arse.

Exchange your robe even for a day
with the raiment of one made of clay.
Lay down your harp and dig these pipes I play.

I'll put my lips to the weeping reeds
till temptation thrills the heart of every hill
and the very stones begin the dance of leaves
as if stones had gained a fluttering will.

Welcome ye cherubs to the carnal hubbub.
Take a break from heaven's eternal monotone.
Inhabit the splendid risk of flesh and bone.

JOHN AGARD (*b.* 1949)

from The Rubaiyat of Omar Khayyam

Ah, my Belovèd, fill the cup that clears
Today of past Regrets and future Fears –
    Tomorrow? – Why, Tomorrow I may be
Myself with Yesterday's Sev'n Thousand Years.

OMAR KHAYYAM (*d.* ?1122)
version by Edward Fitzgerald

The Young May Moon
(AIR: *The Irish Wedding*)

The young May moon is beaming, love,
The glowworm's lamp is gleaming, love,
How sweet to rove thro' Morna's grove,
While the drowsy world is dreaming, love!
Then awake! the heav'ns look bright, my dear!
'Tis never too late for delight, my dear!
And the best of all ways
To lengthen our days,
Is to steal a few hours from the night, my dear!

Now all the world is sleeping, love,
But the Sage, his star-watch keeping, love,
And I whose star, more glorious far,
Is the eye from that casement peeping, love.
Then awake! – till rise of sun, my dear,
The Sage's glass we'll shun, my dear,
Or in watching the flight
Of bodies of light,
He might happen to take thee for one, my dear.

THOMAS MOORE (1779-1852)

Song

   Go lovely Rose,
Tell her that wastes her time and me,
   That now she knows
When I resemble her to thee
   How sweet and fair she seems to be.

   Tell her that's young,
And shuns to have her graces spy'd
   That hadst thou sprung
In desarts where no men abide,
   Thou must have uncommended dy'd.

Small is the worth
Of beauty from the light retir'd;
  Bid her come forth,
Suffer her self to be desir'd,
  And not blush so to be admir'd.

  Then die that she,
The common fate of all things rare
  May read in thee
How small a part of time they share,
  That are so wondrous sweet and fair.

EDMUND WALLER (1606-87)

To His Coy Mistress

Had we but world enough, and time,
This coyness, Lady, were no crime.
We would sit down, and think which way
To walk, and pass our long love's day.
Thou by the Indian Ganges' side
Shouldst rubies find: I by the tide
Of Humber would complain. I would
Love you ten years before the flood:
And you should, if you please, refuse
Till the conversion of the Jews.
My vegetable love should grow
Vaster than empires, and more slow.
An hundred years should go to praise
Thine eyes, and on thy forehead gaze.
Two hundred to adore each breast:
But thirty thousand to the rest.
An age at least to every part,
And the last age should show your heart:
For, Lady, you deserve this state;
Nor would I love at lower rate.

But at my back I always hear
Time's wingèd chariot hurrying near:
And yonder all before us lie
Deserts of vast eternity.
Thy beauty shall no more be found;
Nor, in thy marble vault, shall sound
My echoing song: then worms shall try
That long-preserved virginity:
And your quaint honour turn to dust;
And into ashes all my lust.
The grave's a fine and private place,
But none, I think, do there embrace.
    Now, therefore, while the youthful glue
Sits on thy skin like morning dew,
And while thy willing soul transpires
At every pore with instant fires,
Now let us sport us while we may;
And now, like amorous birds of prey,
Rather at once our time devour,
Than languish in his slow-chapped power.
Let us roll all our strength, and all
Our sweetness, up into one ball:
And tear our pleasures with rough strife,
Thorough the iron grates of life.
Thus, though we cannot make our sun
Stand still, yet we will make him run.

ANDREW MARVELL (1621-78)

The Passionate Shepherd to His Love

Come live with me and be my love,
And we will all the pleasures prove
That valleys, groves, hills and fields,
Woods, or steepy mountain yields.

And we will sit upon the rocks,
Seeing the shepherds feed their flocks,
By shallow rivers to whose falls
Melodious birds sing madrigals.

And I will make thee beds of roses
And a thousand fragrant posies,
A cap of flowers, and a kirtle
Embroidered all with leaves of myrtle;

A gown made of the finest wool
Which from our pretty lambs we pull,
Fair linèd slippers for the cold,
With buckles of the purest gold.

A belt of straw and ivy-buds,
With coral clasps and amber studs,
And if these pleasures may thee move,
Come live with me, and be my love.

The shepherds' swains shall dance and sing
For thy delight each May morning
If these delights thy mind may move,
Then live with me, and be my love.

CHRISTOPHER MARLOWE (1564-93)

The Nymph's Reply to the Shepherd

If all the world and love were young,
And truth in every shepherd's tongue,
These pretty pleasures might me move
To live with thee and be thy love.

But Time drives flocks from field to fold,
When rivers rage and rocks grow cold,
And Philomel becometh dumb;
The rest complains of cares to come.

81

The flowers do fade, and wanton fields
To wayward winter reckoning yields;
A honey tongue, a heart of gall,
Is fancy's spring, but sorrow's fall.

Thy gowns, thy shoes, thy beds of roses,
Thy cap, thy kirtle, and thy posies
Soon break, soon wither, soon forgotten,
In folly ripe, in reason rotten.

Thy belt of straw and ivy buds,
Thy coral clasps and amber studs,
All these in me no means can move
To come to thee and be thy love.

But could youth last and love still breed,
Had joys no date, nor age no need,
Then these delights my mind might move
To live with thee and be thy love.

SIR WALTER RALEGH (?1554-1618)

When Sue Wears Red

When Susanna Jones wears red
Her face is like an ancient cameo
Turned brown by the ages.

Come with a blast of trumpets,
      Jesus!

When Susanna Jones wears red
A queen from some time-dead Egyptian night
Walks once again.

Blow trumpets, Jesus!

And the beauty of Susanna Jones in red
Burns in my heart a love-fire sharp like pain.

Sweet silver trumpets,
       Jesus!

LANGSTON HUGHES (1902-67)

from The Song of Solomon

My beloved is white and ruddy, the chiefest among ten thousand.

His head is as the most fine gold, his locks are bushy, and black as a raven.

His eyes are as the eyes of doves by the rivers of waters, washed with milk, and fitly set.

His cheeks are as a bed of spices, as sweet flowers: his lips like lilies, dropping sweet smelling myrrh.

His hands are as gold rings set with the beryl: his belly is as bright ivory overlaid with sapphires.

His legs are as pillars of marble, set upon sockets of fine gold: his countenance is as Lebanon, excellent as the cedars.

His mouth is most sweet: yea, he is altogether lovely. This is my beloved, and this is my friend, O daughters of Jerusalem.

KING JAMES BIBLE

Women Like You

the communal poem – Sigiri Graffiti, 5th century

They do not stir
these ladies of the mountain
do not give us
the twitch of eyelids

                The king is dead

They answer no one
take the hard
rock as lover.
Women like you
make men pour out their hearts

                'Seeing you I want
                no other life'

                'The golden skins have
                caught my mind'

who came here
out of the bleached land
climbed this fortress
to adore the rock
and with the solitude of the air
behind them
              carved an alphabet
whose motive was perfect desire

wanting these portraits of women
to speak
and caress

Hundreds of small verses
by different hands
became one
habit of the unrequited

Seeing you
I want no other life
and turn around
to the sky
and everywhere below
jungle, waves of heat
secular love

Holding the new flowers
a circle of
first finger and thumb
which is a window

to your breast

pleasure of the skin
earring   earring
curl
of the belly
                and the
stone mermaid
stone heart
dry as a flower
on rock
you long eyed women

the golden
drunk swan breasts
lips
the long long eyes

we stand against the sky

I bring you

a flute
from the throat
of a loon

so talk to me
of the used heart

MICHAEL ONDAATJE (*b.* 1943)

Wild strawberries

What I get I bring home to you:
a dark handful, sweet-edged,
dissolving in one mouthful.

I bother to bring them for you
though they're so quickly over,
pulpless, sliding to juice,

a grainy rub on the tongue
and the taste's gone. If you remember
we were in the woods at wild strawberry time

and I was making a basket of dockleaves
to hold what you'd picked,
but the cold leaves unplaited themselves

and slid apart, and again unplaited themselves
until I gave up and ate wild strawberries
out of your hands for sweetness.

I lipped at your palm –
the little salt edge there,
the tang of money you'd handled.

As we stayed in the wood, hidden,
we heard the sound system below us
calling the winners at Chepstow,
faint as the breeze turned.

The sun came out on us, the shade blotches
went hazel: we heard names
bubble like stock-doves over the woods

as jockeys in stained silks gentled
those sweat-dark, shuddering horses
down to the walk.

HELEN DUNMORE (*b.* 1952)

A Note on the Rapture to His true Love

A blue bowl on the table in the dining room
fills with sunlight. From a sunlit room
I watch my neighbor's sugar maple turn
to shades of gold. It's late September. Soon...
Soon as I'm able I intend to turn
to gold myself. Somewhere I've read that soon
they'll have a formula for prime numbers
and once they do, the world's supposed to end
the way my neighbor always said it would –
in fire. I'll bet we'll all be given numbers
divisible by One and by themselves
and told to stand in line the way you would
for prime cuts at the butcher's. In the end,
maybe it's every man for himself.
Maybe it's someone hollering All Hands On
Deck! Abandon Ship! Women and Children First!
Anyway, I'd like to get my hands on
you. I'd like to kiss your eyelids and make love
as if it were our last time, or the first,
or else the one and only form of love
divisible by which I yet remain myself.
Mary, folks are disappearing one by one.
They turn to gold and vanish like the leaves
of sugar maples. But we can save ourselves.
We'll pick our own salvations, one by one,
from a blue bowl full of sunlight until none is left.

THOMAS LYNCH (b. 1948)

The Way Your Sleeping Hand

The way your sleeping hand
still seeks to cup my V-centre
as if it were:

A hand grenade
A briar patch
A goldmine
A worldbank
An agitated fish
A sapodilla
A cosmic calendar
A soft acre

That would somehow
yield enough
to feed the multitude.

GRACE NICHOLS (*b.* 1950)

Revelation

Your love is darkening my star –
the moon is rising in my life.
My hand is not at home in yours.
Your hand is lust –
my hand is longing.

EDITH SÖDERGRAN (1892-1923)
translated from the Finland Swedish by David McDuff

Mistress

Women whose hands know the feel of a baby's head
Push them confidently in among the melons
And their strong brown thumbs side by side,
Beautifully cuticled, feel for give on the crown.

That summer of the hot winds and the fires
The melons were sold split. He held me one
Before we had paid for it, before all the people,
To smell the inside of at its small
Opening fleur-de-lys and we went down
In a river of laughter between the banked stalls
Among all the people swinging our fruit in a net.

He made the cuts but I opened it
And for a moment my hands were a bowl of flames.
I served him cradles and the moons of nursery rhymes
And a family of rocking boats. We ate
And our mouths ran over with luscious smiles.

Then he closed my hands into a fist and held them shut.

DAVID CONSTANTINE (*b.* 1944)

Waking Under a Spruce With My Love

Up the hill the motorcycle climbs, its growl
near now, entering my dream,
and the girl's hair flares

because it's morning, because I have been sleeping
long enough to become one of the muscles
flexed with the world's gristle.

I can feel the sheet luff on my thighs, the emptiness
cool and pleasant inside my body, and time
stops counting the spruce limbs.

I think this must be the silence that love wants to be,
except I can hear a dog barking, a big dog
far away, then his nails gouging dirt,

and I feel myself twist for the power to get free.
The little engine pumps hard, she hangs
on my shoulders, and we are not

going down in grinding of gravel, not this time, we
are filling silence with the two-stroke slide
of the morning and time rattles

like joy in the spruce, in the car-door slammed, jays
spitting out the black, stale hours,
the sun flying over each bump

in the road, touching the essence of each thing until
the world ticks, sighs, glides ahead easy,
slows, turns, and comes hard again.

DAVE SMITH (*b.* 1942)

Having a Coke With You

is even more fun than going to San Sebastian, Irún, Hendaye,
        Biarritz, Bayonne
or being sick to my stomach on the Travesera de Gracia in Barcelona
partly because in your orange shirt you look like a better happier
        St Sebastian
partly because of my love for you, partly because of your love for
        yoghurt

partly because of the fluorescent orange tulips around the birches
partly because of the secrecy our smiles take on before people and statuary
it is hard to believe when I'm with you that there can be anything as still
as solemn as unpleasantly definitive as statuary when right in front of it
in the warm New York 4 o'clock light we are drifting back and forth
between each other like a tree breathing through its spectacles

and the portrait show seems to have no faces in it at all, just paint
you suddenly wonder why in the world anyone ever did them
                                                    I look
at you and I would rather look at you than all the portraits in the world
except possibly for the *Polish Rider* occasionally and anyway it's in
        the Frick
which thank heavens you haven't gone to yet so we can go together
        the first time
and the fact that you move so beautifully more or less takes care of
        Futurism
just as at home I never think of the *Nude Descending a Staircase* or
at a rehearsal a single drawing of Leonardo or Michelangelo that used
        to wow me
and what good does all the research of the Impressionists do them
when they never got the right person to stand near the tree when the
        sun sank
or for that matter Marino Marini when he didn't pick the rider as
        carefully
as the horse
                it seems they were all cheated of some marvellous experience
which is not going to go wasted on me which is why I'm telling you
        about it

FRANK O'HARA (1922-66)

I'll Explain

It's something you say at your peril.
It's something you shouldn't contain.
It's a truth for the dark and a pillow.
Turn out the light and I'll explain.

It's the obvious truth of the morning
Bitten back as the sun turns to rain,
To the rain, to the dark, to the pillow.
Turn out the light and I'll explain.

    It's what I was hoping to tell you.
    It's what I was hoping you'd guess.
    It's what I was hoping you *wouldn't* guess
    Or you wouldn't mind.
    It's a kind
    Of hopelessness.

It's the hope that you hope at your peril.
It's the hope that you fear to attain.
It's the obvious truth of the evening.
Turn out the light and I'll explain.

JAMES FENTON (*b.* 1949)

Her Bed

See'st thou that Cloud as silver cleare.
Plump, soft, and swelling every where?
Tis *Julia's* Bed, and she sleeps there.

ROBERT HERRICK (1591-1674)

6

'Wild Nights – Wild Nights!'

(EMILY DICKINSON)

'Good God, what a night that was'
(from the Greek Anthology)

Good God, what a night that was,
The bed was so soft, and how we clung,
Burning together, lying this way and that,
Our uncontrollable passions
Flowing through our mouths.
If I could only die that way,
I'd say goodbye to the business of living.

PETRONIUS *(1st century)*
translated from the Greek by Kenneth Rexroth

'Wild Nights'

Wild Nights – Wild Nights!
Were I with thee
Wild Nights should be
Our luxury!

Futile – the Winds –
To a Heart in port –
Done with the Compass –
Done with the Chart!

Rowing in Eden –
Ah, the Sea!
Might I but moor – Tonight –
In Thee!

EMILY DICKINSON (1830-96)

Taking Off Emily Dickinson's Clothes

First, her tippet made of tulle,
easily lifted off her shoulders and laid
on the back of a wooden chair.

And her bonnet,
the bow undone with a light forward pull.

Then the long white dress, a more
complicated matter with mother-of-pearl
buttons down the back,
so tiny and numerous that it takes forever
before my hands can part the fabric,
like a swimmer's dividing water,
and slip inside.

You will want to know
that she was standing
by an open window in an upstairs bedroom,
motionless, a little wide-eyed,
looking out at the orchard below,
the white dress puddled at her feet
on the wide-board, hardwood floor.

The complexity of women's undergarments
in nineteenth-century America
is not to be waved off,
and I proceeded like a polar explorer
through clips, clasps, and moorings,
catches, straps, and whalebone stays,
sailing toward the iceberg of her nakedness.

Later, I wrote in a notebook
it was like riding a swan into the night,
but, of course, I cannot tell you everything –
the way she closed her eyes to the orchard,
how her hair tumbled free of its pins,
how there were sudden dashes
whenever we spoke.

What I can tell you is
it was terribly quiet in Amherst
that Sabbath afternoon,
nothing but a carriage passing the house,
a fly buzzing in a windowpane.

So I could plainly hear her inhale
when I undid the very top
hook-and-eye fastener of her corset

and I could hear her sigh when finally it was unloosed,
the way some readers sigh when they realise
that Hope has feathers,
that reason is a plank,
that life is a loaded gun
that looks right at you with a yellow eye.

BILLY COLLINS (*b.* 1941)

Blues

i love a twenty yr old weekends
dig him way down until he's glad.
yeh, i love a twenty yr old weekends
dig him way down until he's glad
you see what my wanting you has
done gone and made me badddddd.

watched for you each evening
stood right outside my do
said i watched for you each evening
stood right outside my do
but you never came in and
i couldn't stand still no mo

what do you do when you need
a man so much it hurt?
i say where do you go when you

need a man so much it hurt?
you make it down to the corner
and start digging in the dirt.

yeh, i love a twenty yr old weekends
dig him way down until he's dry
yeh i love a twenty yr old weekends
dig him way down until he's dry
you see what my needing you
has done gone and made me try.

you see what my needing you
has done gone and made me try.

SONIA SANCHEZ (*b.* 1934)

The Ram

He jangles his keys in the rain
and I follow like a lamb.
His house is as smoky as a dive.
We go straight downstairs to his room.

I lie on his bed and watch him
undress. His orange baseball jacket,
all the way from Ontario,
drops to the floor – THE RAMS, in felt,

arched across the hunky back.
He unzips his calf-length
Star-walkers, his damp black Levi's,
and adjusts his loaded modelling-pouch:

he stands before me in his socks –
as white as bridesmaids,
little daisies, driven snow.
John Wayne watches from the wall

97

beside a shelf-ful of pistols.
Well, he says, *d'you like it?*
All I can think of is Granny,
how she used to shake her head,

when I stood by her bed on Sundays,
so proud in my soap-smelling
special frock, and say *Ah,*
Bless your little cotton socks!

SELIMA HILL (*b.* 1945)

Coupling

On the wall above the bedside lamp
a large crane-fly is jump-starting
a smaller crane-fly – or vice versa.
They do it tail to tail, like Volkswagens:
their engines must be in their rears.

It looks easy enough. Let's try it.

FLEUR ADCOCK (*b.* 1934)

Night and Day

Like the beat beat beat of the tom-tom
When the jungle shadows fall,
Like the tick tick tock of the stately clock
As it stands against the wall,
Like the drip drip drip of the raindrops
When the sum'r show'r is through,
So a voice within me keeps repeating
You – You – You.

Night and day you are the one,
Only you beneath the moon and under the sun,
Whether near to me or far
It's no matter, darling, where you are,
I think of you, night and day.
Day and night, why is it so
That this longing for you follows wherever I go?
In the roaring traffic's boom,
In the silence of my lonely room,
I think of you, night and day.
Night and day under the hide of me
There's an, oh, such a hungry yearning burning inside of me
And its torment won't be through
Till you let me spend my life making love to you
Day and night, night and day.

COLE PORTER (1892-1964)

Aubade

It was the hour of spells and charms.
Right at the crowing of the cock
She turned herself into my arms
And whispered tenderly: 'Unlock
In me the paradise of pleasure;
Now is the hour, and this the key.
Make haste, sweet, to possess each treasure
That searching shall create in me.

'Taste on my lids the tears that float
On the dark iris of my eyes.
Drink deeply from my murmuring throat
The yielded body's inmost cries.
O quickly, before dawn shall break
And day renew its thousand things,
Enter my paradise, touch and take
Your pleasure while the robin sings.'

Our loves were mingled in that hour,
Pure as the robin's piping call,
Scented with mystery like the flower
Of dusk-blue iris by the wall.
Thereafter day, from us renewing
Its eastern fires, drew from their rest
All things that move, their loves pursuing,
While our love slumbered on the breast.

JAMES McAULEY (1917-76)

Marichiko: 'Making love with you'

Making love with you
Is like drinking sea water.
The more I drink
The thirstier I become,
Until nothing can slake my thirst
But to drink the entire sea.

KENNETH REXROTH (1905-82)
"translation" of invented 20th century Japanese poet

Configurations

He gives her all the configurations
of Europe.

She gives him a cloud burst of parrots.

He gives her straight blond hairs
and a white frenzy.

She gives him black wool. The darkness
of her twin fruits.

He gives her uranium, platinum, aluminium
and concorde.

She gives him her 'Bantu buttocks'.

He rants about the spice in her skin.

She croons his alabaster and scratches him.

He does a Columbus –
falling on the shores of her tangled nappy orchard.

She delivers up the whole Indies again
But this time her wide legs close in
    slowly
Making a golden stool of the empire
of his head.

GRACE NICHOLS (*b*. 1950)

Woman to Man

The eyeless labourer in the night,
the selfless, shapeless seed I hold,
builds for its resurrection day –
silent and swift and deep from sight
foresees the unimagined light.

This is no child with a child's face;
this has no name to name it by:
yet you and I have known it well.
This is our hunter and our chase,
the third who lay in our embrace.

This is the strength that your arm knows,
the arc of flesh that is my breast,
the precise crystals of our eyes.
This is the blood's wild tree that grows
the intricate and folded rose.

101

This is the maker and the made;
this is the question and reply;
the blind head butting at the dark,
the blaze of light along the blade.
Oh hold me, for I am afraid.

JUDITH WRIGHT (1915-2000)

Pentecost

The neighbours hammered on the walls all night,
Outraged by the noise we made in bed.
Still we kept it up until by first light
We'd said everything that could be said.

Undaunted, we began to mewl and roar
As if desire had stripped itself of words.
Remember when we made those sounds before?
When we built a tower heavenwards
They were our reward for blasphemy.
And then again, two thousand years ago,
We huddled in a room in Galilee
Speaking languages we didn't know,
While amethyst uraeuses of flame
Hissed above us. We recalled the tower
And the tongues. We knew this was the same,
But love had turned the curse into a power.

See? It's something that we've always known:
Though we command the language of desire,
The voice of ecstasy is not our own.
We long to lose ourselves amid the choir
Of the salmon twilight and the mackerel sky,
The very air we take into our lungs,
And the rhododendron's cry.

And when you lick the sweat along my thigh,
Dearest, we renew the gift of tongues.

MICHAEL DONAGHY (*b.* 1954)

Act of Love

At night, riding our bed like a willing and dethroned horse,
we are secret depositors proud of our flaws,
flaws that scratch a diamond;
you are a stinging mirror to me, I another to you.
We are each a bird ruthless as cat
but we let that cruelty go into the dark
and lie lithe as lizards, side by side,
our fingernails extracting silver from our hearts,
the distinctive lode we work,
darkness arcing with our buck and doe brights
until we rest for a little, partners slumped on the ropes of night's ring.

Our outstretched arms anchor us, inseparable;
my nipple is hard as diamond, treble and desirous;
my breast-skin soft as unchaperoned moss;
your hand on it a serious shimmer;
my breast grows newer, newer,
my yanked-open laceless nightgown's bodice,
its cotton seam is caught tight around my ribs
where my heart is beating gravely and loudly,
its blood full of steadfast strength and mystery.

The night outside is a teetotal drum we flood into silence
as your delicate hard sex presses against my hip;
when we meet and join we hold our breath,
then breathe out all the burning novelty of our bodies,
a big vapour furling into the room, flag
made from our clear-sky flesh, our unearthly diplomacy,
our hauntingly-real fuck;
I watch my familiar but elaborately-lifted leg
misty and incredulous in the straight-faced dark.

And as we are not blind or dumb
this is the time we stare and cry out best
as we wear out our weariness with thrusting,
our eyes open and glossy, our throats humble with aahs,
sighing into inaudibility, our lips soft reams
of silence; we're giddy with our tongues' work,
as if two serpents had become brother and sister...

As we cast ourselves into the night and the act,
our smooth knuckles shine,

we are gasping as we smell the sleep to come,
waiting for us beyond this untraceable room;
now we clamber the summit of old-friend mountain,
rising faster in our clamour,
swinging locked-together in our bell-apple nakedness,
in the double-pink hammock of the night
made of touch and breath,
(the purposes of the engineering!),
a labour of love as we rush towards that trembling edge,
toppling over yelling into the fall, the rapids,
the waters we enter, fluid as them,
my sex hot and hidden, perfect and full,
the corner of our sinews turned,
a clear answer found, its affirmative leaping from our mouths,
my body's soft freight shaking and accepting
in the clairvoyance of orgasm,
and your answering sheer plunge from mountaintop
into river,
flowing where the bed was.

Sleep takes us then and drops us into its diocese,
drops us from night's peak into a dawn
of martial ardour, of trees mad
with old-clothes spite, a morning
where the starving still wait for us,
each with their lonely cloudy gaze.

So only the sugars of the night offer us any breakfast,
only our night's act of love feeds us,
the remembrance of our bodies like slow-moving turtles
lifted from the sweetness of a sea of honey,
flying into more sweetness.
Only the touchwood of our sweet bed
dams the savage sour torrent of the day.

In the morning we must say goodbye, not hello,
goodbye until the untouchable day has gone
and the night recalls us again to our study,
to our sweating gypsy-wagon sheets,
our navaho pillows and rich pastures,
the mintage of our wild skins.

PENELOPE SHUTTLE (*b.* 1947)

The Good Morrow

I wonder by my troth, what thou, and I
   Did, till we loved? were we not weaned till then,
But sucked on country pleasures, childishly?
   Or snorted we in the seven sleepers' den?
'Twas so; but this, all pleasures fancies be.
If ever any beauty I did see,
Which I desired, and got, 'twas but a dream of thee.

And now good morrow to our waking souls,
   Which watch not one another out of fear;
For love, all love of other sights controls,
   And makes one little room, an every where.
Let sea-discoverers to new worlds have gone,
Let maps to others, worlds on worlds have shown,
Let us possess one world, each hath one, and is one.

My face in thine eye, thine in mine appears,
   And true plain hearts do in the faces rest,
Where can we find two better hemispheres
   Without sharp north, without declining west?
What ever dies, was not mixed equally;
If our two loves be one, or, thou and I
Love so alike, that none do slacken, none can die.

JOHN DONNE (1572-1631)

Plucking the Rushes

A boy and girl are sent to gather rushes for thatching

Green rushes with red shoots,
Long leaves bending to the wind –
You and I in the same boat
Plucking rushes at the Five Lakes.
We started at dawn from the orchid-island:
We rested under the elms till noon.
You and I plucking rushes
Had not plucked a handful when night came!

ANONYMOUS (*4th century*)
translated from the Chinese by Arthur Waley

from The Song of Solomon

I am the rose of Sharon, and the lily of the valleys.

As the lily among thorns, so is my love among the daughters.

As the apple tree among the trees of the wood, so is my beloved
among the sons. I sat down under his shadow with great delight,
and his fruit was sweet to my taste.

He brought me to the banqueting house, and his banner over me
was love.

Stay me with flagons, comfort me with apples: for I am sick of
love.

His left hand is under my head, and his right hand doth embrace
me.

I charge you, O ye daughters of Jerusalem, by the roes, and by
the hinds of the field, that ye stir not up, nor awake my love, till
he please.

The voice of my beloved! behold, he cometh leaping upon the
mountains, skipping upon the hills.

My beloved is like a roe or a young hart: behold, he standeth
behind our wall, he looketh forth at the windows, shewing himself
through the lattice.

My beloved spake, and said unto me, Rise up, my love, my fair
one, and come away.

For, lo, the winter is past, the rain is over and gone;

The flowers appear on the earth; the time of the singing of birds is come, and the voice of the turtle is heard in our land;

The fig tree putteth forth her green figs, and the vines with the tender grape give a good smell. Arise, my love, my fair one, and come away.

O my dove, that art in the clefts of the rock, in the secret places of the stairs, let me see thy countenance, let me hear thy voice; for sweet is thy voice, and thy countenance is comely.

Take us the foxes, the little foxes, that spoil the vines: for our vines have tender grapes.

My beloved is mine, and I am his: he feedeth among the lilies.

Until the day break, and the shadows flee away, turn, my beloved, and be thou like a roe or a young hart upon the mountains of Bether.

KING JAMES BIBLE

Freedom of Love

My wife with the hair of a wood fire
With the thoughts of heat lightning
With the waist of an hourglass
With the waist of an otter in the teeth of a tiger
My wife with the lips of a cockade and of a bunch of stars of the
        last magnitude
With the teeth of tracks of white mice on the white earth
With the tongue of rubbed amber and glass
My wife with the tongue of a stabbed host
With the tongue of a doll that opens and closes its eyes
With the tongue of an unbelievable stone
My wife with the eyelashes of strokes of a child's writing
With brows of the edge of a swallow's nest
My wife with the brow of slates of a hothouse roof
And of steam on the panes
My wife with shoulders of champagne
And of a fountain with dolphin-heads beneath the ice
My wife with wrists of matches
My wife with fingers of luck and ace of hearts
With fingers of mown hay
My wife with armpits of marten and of beechnut

And of Midsummer Night
Of privet and of an angelfish nest
With arms of seafoam and of riverlocks
And of a mingling of the wheat and the mill
My wife with legs of flares
With the movements of clockwork and despair
My wife with calves of eldertree pith
My wife with feet of initials
With feet of rings of keys and Java sparrows drinking
My wife with a neck of unpearled barley
My wife with a throat of the valley of gold
Of a tryst in the very bed of the torrent
With breasts of night
My wife with breasts of a marine molehill
My wife with breasts of the ruby's crucible
With breasts of the rose's spectre beneath the dew
My wife with the belly of an unfolding of the fan of days
With the belly of a gigantic claw
My wife with the back of a bird fleeing vertically
With a back of quicksilver
With a back of light
With a nape of rolled stone and wet chalk
And of the drop of a glass where one has just been drinking
My wife with hips of a skiff
With hips of a chandelier and of arrow-feathers
And of shafts of white peacock plumes
Of an insensible pendulum
My wife with buttocks of sandstone and asbestos
My wife with buttocks of swans' backs
My wife with buttocks of spring
With the sex of an iris
My wife with the sex of a mining-placer and of a platypus
My wife with a sex of seaweed and ancient sweetmeat
My wife with a sex of mirror
My wife with eyes full of tears
With eyes of purple panoply and of a magnetic needle
My wife with savanna eyes
My wife with eyes of water to be drunk in prison
My wife with eyes of wood always under the axe
My wife with eyes of water-level of air earth and fire

ANDRÉ BRETON (1896-1966)
translated from the French by Edouard Roditi

from By Grand Central Station
I Sat Down and Wept

Our passion by the ice pond forced the sun into sight. It has rocked orphans to sleep and thickened the heart of the new-made cabinboy. Heathcliff's look bored a hole through England which generations of heather on the wild moor never erased.

Give me my faith in the one fact, and I can cure cancer and gossip and war. Give me the fact, and then I would cut off my hands and give them to her to comfort her for an hour.

Injure me, betray me, but only make me sure of the love, for all day and all night, away from him and with him, everywhere and always, that is my gravity, and the apples (which ben ripe in my gardayne) fall only towards that.

ELIZABETH SMART (1913-86)

Lovesong

He loved her and she loved him
His kisses sucked out her whole past and future or tried to
He had no other appetite
She bit him she gnawed him she sucked
She wanted him complete inside her
Safe and sure forever and ever
Their little cries fluttered into the curtains

Her eyes wanted nothing to get away
Her looks nailed down his hands his wrists his elbows
He gripped her hard so that life
Should not drag her from that moment
He wanted all future to cease
He wanted to topple with his arms round her
Off that moment's brink and into nothing
Or everlasting or whatever there was
Her embrace was an immense press
To print him into her bones

His smiles were the garrets of a fairy palace
Where the real world would never come
Her smiles were spider bites
So he would lie still till she felt hungry
His words were occupying armies
Her laughs were an assassin's attempts
His looks were bullets daggers of revenge
Her glances were ghosts in the corner with horrible secrets
His whispers were whips and jackboots
Her kisses were lawyers steadily writing
His caresses were the last hooks of a castaway
Her love-tricks were the grinding of locks
And their deep cries crawled over the floors
Like an animal dragging a great trap

His promises were the surgeon's gag
Her promises took the top off his skull
She would get a brooch made of it
His vows pulled out all her sinews
He showed her how to make a love-knot
Her vows put his eyes in formalin
At the back of her secret drawer
Their screams stuck in the wall
Their heads fell apart into sleep like the two halves
Of a lopped melon, but love is hard to stop

In their entwined sleep they exchanged arms and legs
In their dreams their brains took each other hostage

In the morning they wore each other's face

TED HUGHES (1930-98)

The Ecstasy

Where, like a pillow on a bed,
    A pregnant bank swelled up, to rest
The violet's reclining head,
    Sat we two, one another's best;

Our hands were firmly cemented
    With a fast balm, which thence did spring,
Our eye-beams twisted, and did thread
    Our eyes, upon one double string;

So to' intergraft our hands, as yet
    Was all our means to make us one,
And pictures in our eyes to get
    Was all our propagation.

As 'twixt two equal armies, Fate
    Suspends uncertain victory,
Our souls, (which to advance their state,
    Were gone out), hung 'twixt her, and me.

And whilst our souls negotiate there,
    We like sepulchral statues lay;
All day, the same our postures were,
    And we said nothing, all the day.

If any, so by love refined,
    That he soul's language understood,
And by good love were grown all mind,
    Within convenient distance stood,

He (though he knew not which soul spake
    Because both meant, both spake the same)
Might thence a new concoction take,
    And part far purer than he came.

This ecstasy doth unperplex
    (We said) and tell us what we love,
We see by this, it was not sex,
    We see, we saw not what did move:

But as all several souls contain
   Mixture of things, they know not what,
Love, these mixed souls doth mix again,
   And makes both one, each this and that.

A single violet transplant,
   The strength, the colour, and the size,
(All which before was poor, and scant,)
   Redoubles still, and multiplies.

When love, with one another so
   Interinanimates two souls,
The abler soul, which thence doth flow,
   Defects of loneliness controls.

We then, who are this new soul, know,
   Of what we are composed, and made,
For, th' atomies of which we grow,
   Are souls, whom no change can invade.

But O alas, so long, so far
   Our bodies why do we forbear?
They are ours, though they are not we, we are
   The intelligences, they the sphere.

We owe them thanks, because they thus,
   Did us, to us, at first convey,
Yielded their forces, sense, to us,
   Nor are dross to us, but allay.

On man heaven's influence works not so,
   But that it first imprints the air,
So soul into the soul may flow,
   Though it to body first repair.

As our blood labours to beget
   Spirits, as like souls as it can,
Because such fingers need to knit
   That subtle knot, which makes us man:

So must pure lovers' souls descend
   T' affections, and to faculties,
Which sense may reach and apprehend,
   Else a great prince in prison lies.

To our bodies turn we then, that so
   Weak men on love revealed may look;
Love's mysteries in souls do grow,
   But yet the body is his book.

And if some lover, such as we,
   Have heard this dialogue of one,
Let him still mark us, he shall see
   Small change, when we'are to bodies gone.

JOHN DONNE (1572-1631)

The Cinnamon Peeler

If I were a cinnamon peeler
I would ride your bed
and leave the yellow bark dust
on your pillow.

Your breast and shoulders would reek
you could never walk through markets
without the profession of my fingers
floating over you. The blind would
stumble certain of whom they approached
though you might bathe
under rain gutters, monsoon.

Here on the upper thigh
at this smooth pasture
neighbour to your hair
or the crease
that cuts your back. This ankle.
You will be known among strangers
as the cinnamon peeler's wife.

I could hardly glance at you
before marriage
never touch you
– your keen nosed mother, your rough brothers.
I buried my hands
in saffron, disguised them
over smoking tar,
helped the honey gatherers...

When we swam once
I touched you in water
and our bodies remained free,
you could hold me and be blind of smell.
You climbed the bank and said

                this is how you touch other women
the grass cutter's wife, the lime burner's daughter.
And you searched your arms
for the missing perfume

                and knew

                what good is it
to be the lime burner's daughter
left with no trace
as if not spoken to in the act of love
as if wounded without the pleasure of a scar.

You touched
your belly to my hands
in the dry air and said
I am the cinnamon
peeler's wife. Smell me.

MICHAEL ONDAATJE (*b.* 1943)

Ballygrand Widow

So, you have gone my erstwhile glad boy,
whose body, I remember, stained my big cream bed,
and didn't we mix the day and the night in our play,
we never got up for a week.

If I must set my alarm again,
and feed the hungry hens in the yard,
and draw the milk from my cow on time,
and skulk my shame down Ballygrand Street
to get a drink,
it'll not be for you I think,
but my next husband,
a fine cock he shall be.

So, you are no more in this town
my lovely schoolboy, and how the floss
of your chin tickled me.
And you swam your hands all over,
you shouted for joy, the first time.
Ah, my darling!

I wear your mother's spit on my shoes,
the black crow priest has been to beat me.
But you gave me a belly full, the best,
and they shan't take it.
The days are unkind after you, they are empty.
I lie in the sheets, the very same sheets;
you smelled sweeter than meadow hay.
My beautiful boy you have killed me.

DEBORAH RANDALL (*b.* 1957)

Homecoming

By plane, bus and forced march
Across a city after midnight
With nothing to guide me but what you'd called
Your candlelit window amid the electric ones
(But the phone was cracked and the tone was poor.
And perhaps I hadn't heard aright).
I reached a house and struck a light
To read what was chalked beside the bell:
'Once for the Captain, twice for Sue.'
Three times I pressed;
Give me a minute to catch my breath
Before you open, whoever you are.

FRANCIS STUART (1902-2000)

Spilt Milk

Two soluble aspirins spore in this glass, their mycelia
fruiting the water, which I twist into milkiness.
The whole world seems to slide into the drain by my window.

It has rained and rained since you left, the streets black
and muscled with water. Out of pain and exhaustion you came
into my mouth, covering my tongue with your good and bitter milk.

Now I find you have cashed that cheque. I imagine you
slipping the paper under steel and glass. I sit here in a circle
of lamplight, studying women of nine hundred years past.

My hand moves into darkness as I write, *The adulterous woman
lost her nose and ears; the man was fined*. I drain the glass.
I still want to return to that hotel room by the station

to hear all night the goods trains coming and leaving.

SARAH MAGUIRE (*b.* 1957)

The Wandering Islands

You cannot build bridges between the wandering islands;
The Mind has no neighbours, and the unteachable heart
Announces its armistice time after time, but spends
Its love to draw them closer and closer apart.

They are not on the chart; they turn indifferent shoulders
On the island-hunters; they are not afraid
Of Cook or De Quiros, nor of the empire-builders;
By missionary bishops and the tourist trade

They are not annexed; they claim no fixed position;
They take no pride in a favoured latitude;
The committee of atolls inspires in them no devotion
And the earthquake belt no special attitude.

A refuge only for the shipwrecked sailor;
He sits on the shore and sullenly masturbates,
Dreaming of rescue, the pubs in the ports of call or
The big-hipped harlots at the dockyard gates.

But the wandering islands drift on their own business,
Incurious whether the whales swim round or under,
Investing no fear in ultimate forgiveness.
If they clap together, it is only casual thunder

And yet they are hurt – for the social polyps never
Girdle their bare shores with a moral reef;
When the icebergs grind them they know both beauty and terror;
They are not exempt from ordinary grief;

And the sudden ravages of love surprise
Them like acts of God – its irresistible function
They have never treated with convenient lies
As a part of geography or an institution.

An instant of fury, a bursting mountain of spray,
They rush together, their promontories lock,
An instant the castaway hails the castaway,
But the sounds perish in that earthquake shock.

And then, in the crash of ruined cliffs, the smother
And swirl of foam, the wandering islands part.
But all that one mind ever knows of another,
Or breaks the long isolation of the heart,

Was in that instant. The shipwrecked sailor senses
His own despair in a retreating face.
Around him he hears in the huge monotonous voices
Of wave and wind: 'The Rescue will not take place.'

A.D. HOPE (1907-2000)

Dream Songs, *142*

The animal moment, when   he sorted out her tail
in a rump session with the vivid hostess
whose guests had finally gone,
was stronger, though so limited, though failed
all normal impulse before her interdiction, yes,
and Henry gave in.

I'd like to have your baby, but, she moaned,
I'm married. Henry muttered to himself
So am I and was glad
to keep chaste. If this lady he had had
scarcely could he have have ever forgiven himself
and how would he have atoned?

– Mr Bones, you strong on moral these days, hey?
It's good to be faithful but it ain't natural,
as you knows.
– I knew what I knew when I knew when I was astray,
all those bright painful years, forgiving all
but when Henry & his wives came to blows.

JOHN BERRYMAN (1914-72)

The Lover

When she stopped by, just passing, on her way back from picking up
     the kids at school,
taking them to dance, just happened by the business her husband
     owned and her lover worked in,
their glances, hers and the lover's, that is, not the husband's, seemed
     so decorous, so distant,
barely, just barely touching their fiery wings, their clanging she thought
     so well muffled,
that later, in the filthy women's bathroom, in the stall, she was hor-
     rified to hear two typists
coming from the office laughing, about them, all of them, their boss,
     her husband, 'the blind pig,'
one said, and laughed, 'and her, the horny bitch,' the other said, and
     they both laughed again,
'and *him*, did you see *him*, that sanctimonious, lying bastard – I
     thought he was going to *blush*.'

C.K. WILLIAMS (*b.* 1936)

'Th'expense of spirit in a waste of shame'

Th'expense of spirit in a waste of shame
Is lust in action, and, till action, lust
Is perjured, murd'rous, bloody, full of blame,
Savage, extreme, rude, cruel, not to trust,
Enjoyed no sooner but despisèd straight,
Past reason hunted, and no sooner had,
Past reason hated as a swallowed bait
On purpose laid to make the taker mad;
Mad in pursuit, and in possession so,
Had, having, and in quest to have, extreme,
A bliss in proof, and proved, a very woe,
Before, a joy proposed, behind, a dream.
    All this the world well knows, yet none knows well
    To shun the heaven that leads men to this hell.

WILLIAM SHAKESPEARE (1564-1616)

Vegetable Love

I'd like to say the fridge
was clean, but look at the rusty
streaks down the back wall
and the dusty brown pools
underneath the salad crisper.

And this is where I've lived
the past two weeks, since I was pulled
from the vegetable garden.
I'm wild for him: I want to stay crunchy
enough to madden his hard palate and his tongue,
every sensitive part inside his mouth.
But almost hour by hour now, it seems,
I can feel my outer leaves losing resistance,
as oxygen leaks in, water leaks out
and the same tendency creeps further
and further towards my heart.

Down here there's not much action,
just me and another, even limper, lettuce
and half an onion. The door opens so many,
so many times a day, but he never looks
in the salad drawer where I'm curled in a corner.

There's an awful lot of meat. Strange cuts:
whole limbs with their grubby hair,
wings and thighs of large birds,
claws and beaks. New juice
gathers pungency as it rolls down
through the smelly strata of the refrigerator,
and drips on to our fading heads.

The thermostat is kept as low as it will go,
and when the weather changes
for the worse, what's nearest
to the bottom of the fridge starts to freeze.
Three times we've had cold snaps,
and I've felt the terrifying pain
as ice crystals formed at my fringes.

Insulation isn't everything in here:
you've got to relax into the cold,
let it in at every pore. It's proper
for food preservation. But I heat up
again at the thought of him,
at the thought of mixing into one juice
with his saliva, of passing down his throat
and being ingested with the rest
into his body cells where I'll learn
by osmosis another lovely version
of curl, then shrivel, then open again to desire.

JO SHAPCOTT (*b.* 1953)

John Anderson, My Jo

John Anderson, my jo, John,
    I wonder what you mean
To lie so long i' the morning
    And sit so late at e'en?
You'll blear a' your een, John,
    And why do you so?
Come sooner to your bed at e'en,
    John Anderson, my jo.

John Anderson, my jo, John,
    When first that you began,
You had as good a tail-tree
    As any other man;
But now it's waxen wan, John,
    And wrinkles to and fro,
And oft requires my helping hand.
    John Anderson, my jo.

When we were young and yauld, John
   We've lain out-owre the dyke,
And O! it was a fine thing
   To see your hurdies fyke;
To see your hurdies fyke, John,
   And strike the rising blow,
'Twas then I liked your chanter-pipe,
   John Anderson, my jo.

John Anderson, my jo, John,
   You're welcome when you please;
It's either in the warm bed,
   Or else above the claes.
Do you your part above, John,
   And trust to me below,
I've two gae-ups for your gae-down,
   John Anderson, my jo.

When you come on before, John
   See that you do your best;
When I begin to hold you,
   See that you grip me fast;
See that you grip me fast, John,
   Until that I cry 'O!'
Your back shall crack, or I do that,
   John Anderson, my jo.

I'm backed like a salmon,
   I'm breasted like a swan,
My womb is like a down-cod,
   My waist you well may span;
My skin from tip to toe, John,
   Is like the new fa'n snow
And it's all for your conveniency,
   John Anderson, my jo.

ANONYMOUS

een: eyes; *yauld:* strong, vigorous; *hurdies fyke:* buttocks wiggle; *down-cod:*
feather pillow.

Flame and Water

She steams him up
she makes him hot
she makes him rage
he boils over
he floods her
he extinguishes her

She regathers
she heats him
she makes him vapour
he regathers
he sprays her
he makes her smoulder

She regathers
she stings him steadily
she leaves him to cool
he regathers
he keeps up
steady drops on her flame

She warms him he wets her
She warms him he wets her
they carry on
and carry on
wishing for the secret
of balance

JAMES BERRY (*b.* 1924)

Earth and Air

She holds him
she makes him sour
she goes to sleep
he freezes her
he keeps her there
keeps her halfdead

He rouses
he rushes her
refreshes her and shatters her
she holds him
she contains him
she makes him dank

He blows
he flows
he makes her open up
she holds him
she absorbs him
she swallows him

He showers her
in scents
in seeds
she holds him
and blends him
into growing life

JAMES BERRY (*b.* 1924)

At the Time

Perhaps the daring made it
Seem all right. Or
The memory of the daring.
At the time, there were
The midges, was the fidgeting
Of bottles in someone's
Crates; all the mere
Ungainliness of limbs:
There was the wanting
To get it done and over,
And to resume a proper,
Acceptable posture.
Only much afterwards, was there
The having done, was there
That person (think of it),
And that place; all the daring
Shame of it. Only afterwards,
That. There was, really,
Nothing at all of this,
Nothing at all, at the time.

ALAN BROWNJOHN (*b.* 1931)

A Pity. We Were Such a Good Invention

They amputated
Your thighs off my hips
As far as I'm concerned
They are all surgeons. All of them.

They dismantled us
Each from the other.
As far as I'm concerned
They are all engineers. All of them.

A pity. We were such a good
And loving invention.
An aeroplane made from a man and wife.
Wings and everything.
We hovered a little above the earth.

We even flew a little.

YEHUDA AMICHAI (1924-2000)
*translated from the Hebrew by Assia Gutmann & Harold Schimmel
with the collaboration of Ted Hughes*

Swans Mating

Even now I wish that you had been there
Sitting beside me on the riverbank:
The cob and his pen sailing in rhythm
Until their small heads met and the final
Heraldic moment dissolved in ripples.

This was a marriage and a baptism,
A holding of breath, nearly a drowning,
Wings spread wide for balance where he trod,
Her feathers full of water and her neck
Under the water like a bar of light.

MICHAEL LONGLEY (*b.* 1939)

7

'How do I love thee?'

(ELIZABETH BARRETT BROWNING)

from The Rubaiyat of Omar Khayyam

Here with a Loaf of Bread beneath the Bough,
A Flask of Wine, a Book of Verse – and Thou
   Beside me singing in the Wilderness –
And Wilderness is Paradise enow.

OMAR KHAYYAM (*d.* ?1122)
version by Edward Fitzgerald

Celia Celia

When I am sad and weary
When I think all hope has gone
When I walk along High Holborn
I think of you with nothing on

ADRIAN MITCHELL (*b.* 1932)

Alisoun

Bitwene Mersh and Averil,
   When spray biginneth to springe,
The lutel fowl hath hire wil
   On hire lud to singe.
   Ich libbe in love-longinge
For semlokest of alle thinge;
He may me blisse bringe:
   Ich am in hire baundoun.
An hendy hap ichabbe yhent;
Ichot from hevene it is me sent;
From alle wimmen my love is lent,
   And light on Alisoun.

On heu hire her is fair ynogh,
  Hire browe browne, hire eye blake;
With lossum chere he on me logh,
  With middel smal and wel ymake.
  Bote he me wolle to hire take,
  For te buen hire owen make,
  Longe to liven ichulle forsake,
    And feye fallen adown.

Nightes when I wende and wake,
  Forthy min wonges waxeth won;
Levedy, al for thine sake
  Longinge is ylent me on.
  In world nis non so witer mon
  That al hire bounte telle con;
  Hire swire is whittore then the swon,
    And feirest may in towne.

Ich am for wowing al forwake,
  Wery so water in wore,
Lest eny reve me my make;
  Ichabbe y-yirned yore:
  Betere is tholien while sore
  Then mournen evermore.
  Geinest under gore,
    Herkne to my roun:
  An hendy hap ichabbe yhent;
  Ichot from hevene it is me sent;
  From alle wimmen my love is lent,
    And light on Alisoun.

ANONYMOUS (c. 1300)

on hire lud: in her language; semlokest: fairest; baundoun: control; lossum chere:
lovely face; logh: smiled; feye: dead; wonges: cheeks; witer: clever; swire: neck;
tholien: pain; geinest under gore: most gracious under gown; roun: voice; hendy:
lucky; lent: taken away.

The Lovely Étan

I don't know who it is
that Étan is going to sleep with.
But I know the lovely Étan
will not be sleeping alone.

ANONYMOUS *(9th century)*
translated from the Irish by Thomas Kinsella

From the Irish

According to Dinneen, a Gael unsurpassed
In lexicographical enterprise, the Irish
For moon means the white circle in a slice
Of half-boiled potato or turnip; a star
Is the mark on the forehead of a beast
And the sun is the bottom of a lake, or well.

Well, if I say to you your face
Is like a slice of half-boiled turnip,
Your hair is the colour of a lake's bottom
And at the centre of each of your eyes
Is the mark of the beast, it is because
I want to love you properly, according to Dinneen.

IAN DUHIG *(b. 1954)*

Apology for Understatement

Forgive me that I pitch your praise too low.
Such reticence my reverence demands,
For silence falls with laying on of hands.

Forgive me that my words come thin and slow.
This could not be a time for eloquence,
For silence falls with healing of the sense.

We only utter what we lightly know.
And it is rather that my love knows me.
It is that your perfection set me free.

Verse is dressed up that has nowhere to go.
You took away my glibness with my fear.
Forgive me that I stand in silence here.

It is not words could pay you what I owe.

JOHN WAIN (1925-94)

'How do I love thee?'
(Sonnets from the Portuguese, XLIII)

How do I love thee? Let me count the ways.
I love thee to the depth and breadth and height
My soul can reach, when feeling out of sight
For the ends of Being and ideal Grace.
I love thee to the level of everyday's
Most quiet need, by sun and candle-light.
I love thee freely, as men strive for Right:
I love thee purely, as they turn from Praise.
I love thee with the passion put to use
In my old griefs, and with my childhood's faith.
I love thee with a love I seemed to lose
With my lost saints! – I love thee with the breath,
Smiles, tears, of all my life! – and, if God choose,
I shall but love thee better after death.

ELIZABETH BARRETT BROWNING (1806-61)

'Fine knacks for ladies'

Fine knacks for ladies, cheape choise brave and new,
Good penniworths but mony cannot move,
I keepe a faier but for the faier to view
A begger may bee liberall of love,
Though all my wares bee trash the hart is true,
                            The hart is true,
                            The hart is true.

Great gifts are guiles and looke for gifts againe,
My trifles come, as treasures from my minde,
It is a precious Jewell to bee plaine,
Sometimes in shell th'orienst pearles we finde,
Of others take a sheafe, of mee a graine,
                        Of mee a graine,
                        Of mee a graine.

Within this packe pinnes points laces and gloves,
And divers toies fitting a country faier,
But in my hart where duety serves and loves,
Turtels and twins, courts brood, a heavenly paier,
Happy the hart that thincks of no removes,
                        Of no removes,
                        Of no removes.

JOHN DOWLAND (1563-1626)

knacks: trinkets; *orienst:* brilliant.

'Shall I compare thee to a summer's day?'

Shall I compare thee to a summer's day?
Thou art more lovely and more temperate.
Rough winds do shake the darling buds of May,
And summer's lease hath all too short a date.
Sometime too hot the eye of heaven shines,
And often is his gold complexion dimmed;
And every fair from fair sometime declines,
By chance or nature's changing course untrimmed.
But thy eternal summer shall not fade,
Nor lose possession of that fair thou ow'st,
Nor shall Death brag thou wand'rest in his shade,
When in eternal lines to time thou grow'st.
   So long as men can breathe or eyes can see,
   So long lives this, and this gives life to thee.

WILLIAM SHAKESPEARE (1564-1616)

He Wishes for the Cloths of Heaven

Had I the heavens' embroidered cloths,
Enwrought with golden and silver light,
The blue and the dim and the dark cloths
Of night and light and the half-light,
I would spread the cloths under your feet:
But I, being poor, have only my dreams;
I have spread my dreams under your feet;
Tread softly because you tread on my dreams.

W.B. YEATS (1865-1939)

Cleaning Ashtrays

We were as hung-up on one another as Romeo and Juliet,
Not only in the days of our courtship
But after fifteen years of matrimony
(Only the week before she left me
She held me in her arms on the boat deck
Of the Cork-Swansea Ferry,
Pledging eternal love to one another,
The lifeboats above our heads as solid as ever,
Permanent fixtures – only wholly symbolic);
Yet our love-cries in the night had grown infrequent
And she had multiplied the numbers of cigarettes she smoked.
After she went out to work, and the children to school,
I stood in the kitchen cleaning ashtrays;
The spectacle of a kitchen sink with encrusted ashtrays
Piled-up with tap water dripping into the scum
Made me fear her with a fierce, irrational fear.
As I scoured the ashtrays with my bare fingers
I swore I'd smash these evil receptacles on the kitchen floor
If she'd not mend her ways and give up the fags.
I interpreted each rim of wet black ash
As a personal insult to my individual being
Which she – concerned to ontologically annihilate me –
Had deliberately contrived by continuing to smoke
While reading, to cause me more pain, Jean-Paul Sartre.
What chance had nervous chain-smoking Juliet
When Romeo cleaning ashtrays had such thoughts?
If only Romeo had been more ethical, less romantic,
He might have thought more of love, less of self,
And planted in her lips such petalled fires
As she would have had no need to inhale tobacco.
Now Julietless, how Romeo pines for all those days and nights
Cleaning ashtrays – cleaning ashtrays for his only Juliet.

PAUL DURCAN (*b.*1944)

Calcium

Because I love the very bones of you,
and you are somehow rooted in my bone,
I'll tell you of the seven years

by which the skeleton renews itself,
so that we have the chance to be
a person, now and then, who's

something other than ourselves;
and how the body, if deficient,
will bleed the calcium it needs –

for heart, for liver, spleen –
from bone, which incidentally,
I might add, is not the thorough

structure that you might
suppose, but living tissue which
the doctors say a woman of my age

should nurture mindfully with fruit,
weightbearing exercise, and supplements
to halt the dangers of a fracture when I'm old;

and because I love you I will also tell
how stripped of skin the papery bone
is worthy of inscription, could hold

a detailed record of a navy or a store of grain,
and how, if it's preserved
according to the pharoahs,

wrapped in bandages of coca leaf, tobacco,
it will survive long after all our books,
and even words are weightless;

and perhaps because the heaviness of your head,
the way I love the slow, sweet sense of you,
the easiness by which you're stilled,

how the fleshy structures that your skeleton,
your skull maintain, are easily interrogated,
it reminds me how our hands,

clasped for a moment, now, amount
to everything I have; how even your smile
as it breaks me up, has the quality of ice,

the long lines of loneliness
like a lifetime ploughed across a palm,
the permanence of snow.

DERYN REES-JONES (*b.* 1968)

11 February 1946

I kept searching for you in the stars
When I questioned them as a child.
I asked the mountains for you,
But they gave me solitude and brief peace
Only a few times.
Because you weren't there, in the long evenings
I considered the rash blasphemy
That the world was God's error,
Myself an error in the world.
And when I was face to face with death –
No, I shouted from every fibre.
I hadn't finished yet;
There was still too much to do.
Because you were there before me,
With me beside you, just like today,
A man a woman under the sun.
I came back because you were there.

PRIMO LEVI (1919-87)
translated from the Italian by Ruth Feldman & Brian Swann

The White Word

To you who beat with brightness on my sands
the slounging sunlight of your sea flung word
I bring this morning to be filled or drained away,
to be floated derelict or a gala day.

Set your word's orchard fair to find my ear.
Your tongue has olive branch and burning bush.
O over me can fall the fabulous peace
or scorch of glory sponsor my release.

I listen and the star falls. The white bird
starts up from your breath. And for this space
whale and Orion, earthquake and mustard seed
merge. And the algebra of ocean comes right.
The headlands summon the sea and the fish
    take their places.

NESSIE DUNSMUIR (1909-99)

I Leave This at Your Ear

I leave this at your ear for when you wake.
A creature in its abstract cage asleep.
Your dreams blindfold you by the light they make.

The owl called from the naked-woman tree
As I came down by the Kyle farm to hear
Your house silent by the speaking sea.

I have come late but I have come before
Later with slaked steps from stone to stone
To hope to find you listening for the door.

I stand in the ticking room. My dear, I take
A moth kiss from your breath. The shore gulls cry.
I leave this at your ear for when you wake.

W.S. GRAHAM (1918-86)

Late Air

From a magician's midnight sleeve
    the radio-singers
distribute all their love-songs
over the dew-wet lawns.
    And like a fortune-teller's
their marrow-piercing guesses are whatever you believe.

But on the Navy Yard aerial I find
    better witnesses
for love on summer nights.
Five remote red lights
    keep their nests there; Phoenixes
burning quietly, where the dew cannot climb.

ELIZABETH BISHOP (1911-79)

I Will Give My Love an Apple

I will give my love an apple without e'er a core,
I will give my love a house without e'er a door,
I will give my love a palace wherein she may be,
And she may unlock it without any key.

My head is the apple without e'er a core,
My mind is the house without e'er a door,
My heart is the palace wherein she may be,
And she may unlock it without any key.

ANONYMOUS

Static

The storm shakes out its sheets
against the darkening window:
the glass flinches under thrown hail.
Unhinged, the television slips its hold,
streams into black and white
then silence, as the lines go down.
Her postcards stir on the shelf, tip over;
the lights of Calais trip out one by one.

He cannot tell her
how the geese scull back at twilight,
how the lighthouse walks its beam
across the trenches of the sea.
He cannot tell her how the open night
swings like a door without her,
how he is the lock
and she is the key.

ROBIN ROBERTSON (*b.* 1955)

She Moved Through the Fair

My young love said to me, 'My brothers won't mind,
And my parents won't slight you for your lack of kind.'
Then she stepped away from me, and this she did say,
'It will not be long, love, till our wedding day.'

She stepped away from me and she moved through the fair,
And fondly I watched her go here and go there,
Then she went her way homeward with one star awake,
As the swan in the evening moves over the lake.

The people were saying no two were e'er wed
But one had a sorrow that never was said,
And I smiled as she passed with her goods and her gear,
And that was the last that I saw of my dear.

I dreamt it last night that my young love came in,
So softly she entered, her feet made no din;
She came close beside me, and this she did say,
'It will not be long, love, till our wedding day.'

PADRAIC COLUM (1881-1972)

To one that asked me why I lov'd *J.G.*

Why do I Love? go, ask the Glorious Sun
Why every day it round the world doth Run:
Ask *Thames* and *Tyber*, why the Ebb and Flow:
Ask Damask Roses, why in *June* they blow;
Ask Ice and Hail, the reason, why they're Cold:
Decaying Beauties, why they will grow Old:
They'l tell thee, Fate, that every thing doth move,
Inforces them to this, and me to Love.
There is no Reason for our Love or Hate,
'Tis irresistable, as Death or Fate;
'Tis not his Face; I've sence enough to see,
That is not good, though doated on by me:
Nor is't his Tongue, that has this Conquest won;
For that at least is equall'd by my own:
His Carriage can to none obliging be,
'Tis Rude, Affected, full of Vanity:
Strangely Ill-natur'd, Peevish, and Unkind,
Unconstant, False, to Jealousie inclin'd;
His Temper cou'd not have so great a Pow'r,
'Tis mutable, and changes every hour:
Those vigorous Years that Women so Adore,
Are past in him: he's twice my Age and more;
And yet I love this false, this worthless Man,
With all the Passion that a Woman can;
Doat on his Imperfections, though I spy
Nothing to Love; I Love, and know not why.
Sure 'tis Decreed in the dark Book of Fate,
That I shou'd Love, and he shou'd be ingrate.

'EPHELIA' (*c*.1679)

140

Bog Love

Wee Shemus was a misdropt man
  Without a shoulder to his back;
He had the way to lift a rann
  And throttled rabbits in a sack.

And red-haired Mary, whom he wed,
  Brought him but thirty shillings told;
She had but one eye in her head,
  But Shemus counted it for gold.

The two went singing in the hay
  Or kissing underneath the sloes,
And where they chanced to pass the day
  There was no need to scare the crows.

But now with Mary waked and laid
  As decent as she lived and died,
Poor Shemus went to buy a spade
  To dig himself a place beside.

SHANE LESLIE (1885-1971)

'My Mistress' eyes are nothing like the sun'

My mistress' eyes are nothing like the sun;
Coral is far more red than her lip's red;
If snow be white, why then her breasts are dun;
If hairs be wires, black wires grow on her head.
I have seen roses damasked, red and white,
But no such roses see I in her cheeks,
And in some perfumes is there more delight
Than in the breath that from my mistress reeks.
I love to hear her speak, yet well I know
That music hath a far more pleasing sound.
I grant I never saw a goddess go;
My mistress when she walks treads on the ground.
   And yet, by heaven, I think my love as rare
   As any she belied with false compare.

WILLIAM SHAKESPEARE (1564-1616)

Lonely Love

I love to see those loving and beloved
Whom Nature seems to have spited; unattractive,
Unnoticeable people, whose dry track
No honey-drop of praise, or understanding,
Or bare acknowledgment that they existed,
Perhaps yet moistened. Still, they make their world.

She with her arm in his – O Fate, be kind,
Though late, be kind; let her have never cause
To live outside her dream, nor unadore
This underling in body, mind and type,
Nor part from him what makes her dwarfish form
Take grace and fortune, envy's antitone.

I saw where through the plain a river and road
Ran quietly, and asked no more event
Than sun and rain and wind, and night and day,
Two walking – from what cruel show escaped?
Deformity, defect of mind their portion.
But I forget the rest of that free day of mine,
And in what flowerful coils, what airy music
It led me there and on; those two I see
Who, loving, walking slowly, saw not me,
But shared with me the strangest happiness.

EDMUND BLUNDEN (1896-1974)

'When men shall find thy flower'

When men shall find thy flower, thy glory, pass,
And thou with careful brow, sitting alone,
Receivèd hast this message from thy glass,
That tells the truth and says that all is gone;
Fresh shalt thou see in me the wounds thou mad'st,
Though spent thy flame, in me the heat remaining:
I that have loved thee thus before thou fad'st –
My faith shall wax, when thou art in thy waning.
The world shall find this miracle in me,
That fire can burn when all the matter's spent:
Then what my faith hath been thyself shalt see,
And that thou wast unkind thou mayst repent.
    Thou mayst repent that thou hast scorned my tears,
    When Winter snows upon thy sable hairs.

SAMUEL DANIEL (1562?-1619)

'When forty winters shall besiege thy brow'

When forty winters shall besiege thy brow,
And dig deep trenches in thy beauty's field,
Thy youth's proud livery, so gazed on now,
Will be a tattered weed of small worth held.
Then being asked where all thy beauty lies,
Where all the treasure of thy lusty days,
To say within thine own deep-sunken eyes
Were an all-eating shame and thriftless praise.
How much more praise deserved thy beauty's use
If thou couldst answer 'This fair child of mine
Shall sum my count and make my old excuse,'
Proving his beauty by succession thine.
    This were to be new made when thou art old,
    And see thy blood warm when thou feel'st it cold.

WILLIAM SHAKESPEARE (1564-1616)

'Since she's all winter'
(Sonnets for Helen, 1, 22)

    Since she's all winter, with a heart of snow
Plated in ice and armed with icicles,
And loves me only for these canticles,
I'm mad not to undo my bonds and go.
    What use to me are her great name and race? –
Beautiful prisons, well-bred slavery.
– Mistress, my hair's not gone so grey on me
Another heart won't gladly take your place.

    Love is a child and does not hide the truth:
You may be proud, and rich in beauty too,
But not enough to scorn a heart that's true;
    I can't re-enter April and my youth.
Grey though my head is now, love me today,
And I shall love you when your own is grey.

PIERRE DE RONSARD (1524-85)
translated from the French by Alistair Elliot

In a Bath Teashop

'Let us not speak, for the love we bear one another –
    Let us hold hands and look.'
She, such a very ordinary little woman;
    He, such a thumping crook:
But both, for the moment, little lower than the angels
    In the teashop inglenook.

SIR JOHN BETJEMAN (1906-84)

Giving Potatoes

STRONG MAN: Mashed potatoes cannot hurt you, darling
               Mashed potatoes mean no harm
               I have brought you mashed potatoes
               From my mashed potato farm.

LADY: Take away your mashed potatoes
               Leave them in the desert to dry
               Take them away your mashed potatoes
               You look like shepherd's pie.

BRASH MAN: A packet of chips, a packet of chips,
               Wrapped in the *Daily Mail*,
               Golden juicy and fried for a week
               In the blubber of the Great White Whale.

LADY: Take away your fried potatoes
               Use them to clean your ears
               You can eat your fried potatoes
               With Birds-Eye frozen tears.

OLD MAN:	I have borne this baked potato O'er the Generation Gap. Pray accept this baked potato Let me lay it in your heated lap.
LADY:	Take away your baked potato In your fusty musty van Take away your baked potato You potato-skinned old man.
FRENCHMAN:	She rejected all potatoes For a thousand nights and days Till a Frenchman wooed and won her With pommes de terre Lyonnaises.
LADY:	Oh my corrugated lover So creamy and so brown Let us fly across to Lyons And lay our tubers down.

ADRIAN MITCHELL (*b.* 1932)

'somewhere i have never travelled'

somewhere i have never travelled,gladly beyond
any experience,your eyes have their silence:
in your most frail gesture are things which enclose me,
or which i cannot touch because they are too near

your slightest look easily will unclose me
though i have closed myself as fingers,
you open always petal by petal myself as Spring opens
(touching skilfully,mysteriously)her first rose

or if your wish be to close me,i and
my life will shut very beautifully,suddenly,
as when the heart of this flower imagines
the snow carefully everywhere descending;

nothing which we are to perceive in this world equals
the power of your intense fragility:whose texture
compels me with the colour of its countries,
rendering death and forever with each breathing

(i do not know what it is about you that closes
and opens;only something in me understands
the voice of your eyes is deeper than all roses)
nobody,not even the rain,has such small hands

E.E. CUMMINGS (1894–1962)

The River Merchant's Wife: A Letter

While my hair was still cut straight across my forehead
I played about the front gate, pulling flowers.
You came by on bamboo stilts, playing horse,
You walked about my seat, playing with blue plums.
And we went on living in the village of Chokan:
Two small people, without dislike or suspicion.

At fourteen I married My Lord you.
I never laughed, being bashful.
Lowering my head, I looked at the wall.
Called to, a thousand times, I never looked back.

At fifteen I stopped scowling,
I desired my dust to be mingled with yours
Forever and forever and forever.
Why should I climb the look out?

At sixteen you departed,
You went into far Ku-to-yen, by the river of swirling eddies,
And you have been gone five months.
The monkeys make sorrowful noise overhead.

You dragged your feet when you went out.
By the gate now, the moss is grown, the different mosses,
Too deep to clear them away!
The leaves fall early this autunm, in wind.
The paired butterflies are already yellow with August
Over the grass in the West garden;
They hurt me. I grow older.
If you are coming down through the narrows of the river Kiang,
Please let me know beforehand,
And I will come out to meet you
                                    As far as Cho-fu-Sa.

LI PO (701-62)
version from the Chinese by Ezra Pound

Lullaby

Lay your sleeping head, my love,
Human on my faithless arm;
Time and fevers burn away
Individual beauty from
Thoughtful children, and the grave
Proves the child ephemeral:
But in my arms till break of day
Let the living creature lie,
Mortal, guilty, but to me
The entirely beautiful.

Soul and body have no bounds:
To lovers as they lie upon
Her tolerant enchanted slope
In their ordinary swoon,
Grave the vision Venus sends
Of supernatural sympathy,
Universal love and hope;
While an abstract insight wakes
Among the glaciers and the rocks
The hermit's sensual ecstasy.

Certainty, fidelity
On the stroke of midnight pass
Like vibrations of a bell,
And fashionable madmen raise
Their pedantic boring cry:
Every farthing of the cost,
All the dreaded cards foretell,
Shall be paid, but from this night
Not a whisper, not a thought,
Not a kiss nor look be lost.

Beauty, midnight, vision dies:
Let the winds of dawn that blow
Softly round your dreaming head
Such a day of sweetness show
Eye and knocking heart may bless,
Find the mortal world enough;
Noons of dryness see you fed
By the involuntary powers,
Nights of insult let you pass
Watched by every human love.

W.H. AUDEN (1907-73)

Air for the Witness of a Departure

A high wind blows
over the long white lea
lover
O lover
over the white lea.
Knows
who knows where my love is riding?

Thrush in the maybloom
high winds blow
O
over the long white lea.
Knows
who knows where my love is riding? –
thrush in the maybloom
riding
riding
over the long white lea.

CHRISTOPHER LOGUE (*b.* 1926)

Love Song

My own dear love, he is strong and bold
　　And he cares not what comes after.
His words ring sweet as a chime of gold,
　　And his eyes are lit with laughter.
He is jubilant as a flag unfurled –
　　Oh, a girl, she'd not forget him.
My own dear love, he is all my world –
　　And I wish I'd never met him.

My love, he's mad, and my love, he's fleet,
　　And a wild young wood-thing bore him!
The ways are fair to his roaming feet,
　　And the skies are sunlit for him.
As sharply sweet to my heart he seems
　　As the fragrance of acacia.
My own dear love, he is all my dreams –
　　And I wish he were in Asia.

My love runs by like a day in June,
　　And he makes no friends of sorrows.
He'll tread his galloping rigadoon
　　In the pathway of the morrows.
He'll live his days where the sunbeams start,
　　Nor could storm or wind uproot him.
My own dear love, he is all my heart –
　　And I wish somebody'd shoot him.

DOROTHY PARKER (1893-1967)

'You who never arrived'

You who never arrived
in my arms, Beloved, who were lost
from the start,
I don't even know what songs
would please you. I have given up trying
to recognise you in the surging wave of the next
moment. All the immense
images in me – the far-off, deeply-felt landscape,
cities, towers, and bridges, and un-
suspected turns in the path,
and those powerful lands that were once
pulsing with the life of the gods –
all rise within me to mean
you, who forever elude me.

You, Beloved, who are all
the gardens I have ever gazed at,
longing. An open window
in a country house –, and you almost
stepped out, pensive, to meet me. Streets that I chanced upon, –
you had just walked down them and vanished.
And sometimes, in a shop, the mirrors
were still dizzy with your presence and, startled, gave back
my too-sudden image. Who knows? perhaps the same
bird echoed through both of us
yesterday, separate, in the evening...

RAINER MARIA RILKE (1875-1926)
translated from the German by Stephen Mitchell

8

'I will love thee unto my death'

(JOHN GOWER)

The Beautiful American Word, Sure

The beautiful American word, Sure,
As I have come into a room, and touch
The lamp's button, and the light blooms with such
Certainty where the darkness loomed before,

As I care for what I do not know, and care
Knowing for little she might not have been,
And for how little she would be unseen,
The intercourse of lives miraculous and dear.

Where the light is, and each thing clear,
Separate from all others, standing in its place,
I drink the time and touch whatever's near,

And hope for day when the whole world has that face:
For what assures her present every year?
In dark accidents the mind's sufficient grace.

DELMORE SCHWARTZ (1913-66)

'Bright star, would I were stedfast as thou art'

Bright star, would I were stedfast as thou art —
    Not in lone splendour hung aloft the night,
And watching, with eternal lids apart.
    Like nature's patient, sleepless Eremite.
The moving waters at their priestlike task
    Of pure ablution round earth's human shores,
Or gazing on the new soft-fallen mask
    Of snow upon the mountains and the moors —
No — yet still stedfast, still unchangeable.
    Pillow'd upon my fair love's ripening breast,
To feel for ever its soft swell and fall,
    Awake for ever in a sweet unrest,
Still, still to hear her tender-taken breath,
And so live ever — or else swoon to death.

JOHN KEATS (1795-1821)

Ballad of a Shadow

Take from me my voice and I shall voiceless go
to find you; take from me my face,
I'll treck the hills invisibly,
my strength, and I shall run but keep no pace.

Even in cities, take the sense with which I reason
and I shall seek, but close it in your heart,
keep this and forget this
and this, when we're apart,

will be the shadow game of love.
And I shall love in secret
and I shall love in crowds
and love in darkness, in the quiet

outlet of shadows, and in cities
as a ghost walking unnoticed,
and love with books, using their pages like a wind,
not reading, and with people, latticed

by words but through the lattice loving.
And when at last my love is understood,
with you I shall not love but breathe
and turn by breathing into flesh and blood.

ALICE OSWALD (*b.* 1966)

A Valediction: forbidding Mourning

As virtuous men pass mildly away,
  And whisper to their souls, to go,
Whilst some of their sad friends do say,
  The breath goes now, and some say, no:

So let us melt, and make no noise,
  No tear-floods, nor sigh-tempests move,
'Twere profanation of our joys
  To tell the laity our love.

Moving of th' earth brings harms and fears,
  Men reckon what it did and meant,
But trepidation of the spheres,
  Though greater far, is innocent.

Dull sublunary lovers' love
  (Whose soul is sense) cannot admit
Absence, because it doth remove
  Those things which elemented it.

But we by a love, so much refined,
  That our selves know not what it is,
Inter-assurèd of the mind,
  Care less, eyes, lips, and hands to miss.

Our two souls therefore, which are one,
  Though I must go, endure not yet
A breach, but an expansion,
  Like gold to aery thinness beat.

If they be two, they are two so
  As stiff twin compasses are two,
Thy soul the fixed foot, makes no show
  To move, but doth, it th'other do.

And though it in the centre sit,
  Yet when the other far doth roam,
It leans, and hearkens after it,
  And grows erect, as that comes home.

Such wilt thou be to me, who must
    Like th' other foot, obliquely run;
Thy firmness makes my circle just,
    And makes me end, where I begun.

JOHN DONNE (1572-1631)

Modern Declaration

I, having loved ever since I was a child a few things, never having
        wavered
In these affections; never through shyness in the houses of the rich
        or in the presence of clergymen having denied these loves;
Never when worked upon by cynics like chiropractors having
        grunted or clicked a vertebra to the discredit of these loves;
Never when anxious to land a job having diminished them by a
        conniving smile; or when befuddled by drink
Jeered at them through heartache or lazily fondled the fingers of
        their alert enemies; declare

That I shall love you always.
No matter what party is in power;
No matter what temporary expedient combination of allied interests
        wins the war;
Shall love you always.

EDNA ST VINCENT MILLAY (1892-1950)

'Let me not to the marriage of true minds'

Let me not to the marriage of true minds
Admit impediments; love is not love
Which alters when it alteration finds,
Or bends with the remover to remove.
O, no, it is an ever-fixèd mark
That looks on tempests and is never shaken;
It is the star to every wand'ring bark,
Whose worth's unknown, although his height be taken.
Love's not Time's fool, though rosy lips and cheeks
Within his bending sickle's compass come;
Love alters not with his brief hours and weeks,
But bears it out even to the edge of doom.
    If this be error and upon me proved,
    I never writ, nor no man ever loved.

WILLIAM SHAKESPEARE (1564-1616)

Code Poem

The life that I have is all that I have
And the life that I have is yours.
The love that I have of the life that I have
Is yours and yours and yours.

A sleep I shall have, a rest I shall have,
Yet death will be but a pause,
For the peace of my years in the long green grass
Will be yours and yours and yours.

LEO MARKS (1920-2001)

This poem, written by an intelligence officer, was used as a code for transmitting secret messages and was memorised by Violette Szabo and other British agents working with the French Resistance during the Second World War.

Answer to a Child's Question

Do you ask what the birds say? The Sparrow, the Dove,
The Linnet and Thrush say, 'I love and I love!'
In the winter they're silent – the wind is so strong;
What it says, I don't know, but it sings a loud song.
But green leaves, and blossoms, and sunny warm weather,
And singing, and loving – all come back together.
But the Lark is so brimful of gladness and love,
The green fields below him, the blue sky above,
That he sings, and he sings; and for ever sings he –
'I love my Love, and my Love loves me!'

SAMUEL TAYLOR COLERIDGE (1772-1834)

Song

Out upon it, I have lov'd
   Three whole days together;
And am like to love three more,
   If it prove fair weather.

Time shall moult away his wings,
   Ere he shall discover
In the whole wide world agen
   Such a constant lover.

But the spite on't is, no praise
   Is due at all to me:
Love with me had made no staies,
   Had it any been but she.

Had it any been but she,
   And that very Face,
There had been at least ere this
   A dozen dozen in her place.

SIR JOHN SUCKLING (1609-42)

It is so long ago!

It is so long ago!
How shall the man I now am know
the man I was before you came?
    I have forgot his name
    It was so long ago –
    How shall I know?

It is so long ago
the time when life was faint and low
the time that was not love, you came,
    And call'd me by my name:
    It is so long ago –
    A month or so!

CHRISTOPHER BRENNAN (1870-1932)

'Forget not yet the tried intent'

Forget not yet the tried intent
Of such a truth as I have meant:
My great travail so gladly spent
        Forget not yet.

Forget not yet when first began
The weary life ye know, since whan
The suit, the service none tell can.
        Forget not yet.

Forget not yet the great assays,
The cruel wrong, the scornful ways,
The painful patience in denays.
        Forget not yet.

Forget not yet, forget not this,
How long ago hath been, and is,
The mind that never meant amiss.
        Forget not yet.

Forget not then thine own approved,
The which so long hath thee so loved,
Whose steadfast faith yet never moved:
        Forget not this.

SIR THOMAS WYATT (1503-42)

Meditation on Wyatt II

'Forget not yet, forget not this'
        We are what darkness has become:
        two bodies bathed in saffron light
        disarmed by sudden distances
        pitched on the singing heights of time
        our skin aflame with eastern airs,
        changed beyond reason, but not rhyme.

'The which so long hath thee so loved'
        counting the pulsebeats   foot to foot
        our splendid metres   limb to limb
        sweet assonance of tongue and tongue
        figures of speech to speech   bemused
        with metaphors as unimproved
        as the crooked roads of genius

        but our hearts' rhymes are absolute.

GWEN HARWOOD (1920-95)

One Thing at Least

One thing at least I understood
Practically from the start,
That loving must be learnt by heart
If it's to be any good.

It isn't in the flash of thunder,
But in the silent power to give –
A habit into which we live
Ourselves, and grow to be a wonder.

Some like me are slow to learn:
What's plain can be mysterious still.
Feelings alter, fade, return,

But love stands constant in the will:
It's not alone the touching, seeing,
It's how to mean the other's being.

JAMES McAULEY (1917-76)

'O thou my sorwe and my gladnesse'

O thou my sorwe and my gladnesse,
O thou my hele and my sikenesse,
O thou my wanhope and my trust,
O thou my disese and all my lust,
O thou my wele, O thou my wo,
O thou my frende, O thou my fo,
O thou my love, O thou my hate,
For the mote I be dede algate.
Thilk ende may I nought afterte,
And yet with all min hole herte,
While that there lasteth me any breth,
I woll the love unto my deth.

JOHN GOWER (?1330-1408)

To Althea, From Prison

When Love with unconfined wings
    Hovers within my Gates;
And my divine *Althea* brings
    To whisper at the Grates:
When I lye tangled in her haire,
    And fetterd to her eye;
The *Gods* that wanton in the Aire,
    Know no such Liberty.

When flowing Cups run swiftly round
    With no allaying *Thames*,
Our carelesse heads with Roses bound,
    Our hearts with Loyall Flames;
When thirsty griefe in Wine we steepe,
    When Healths and draughts go free,
Fishes that tipple in the Deepe,
    Know no such Libertie.

When (like committed Linnets) I
    With shriller throat shall sing
The sweetnes, Mercy, Majesty,
    And glories of my KING;
When I shall voyce aloud, how Good
    He is, how Great should be;
Inlarged Winds that curle the Flood,
    Know no such Liberty.

Stone Walls doe not a Prison make,
    Nor Iron bars a Cage;
Minds innocent and quiet take
    That for an Hermitage;
If I have freedome in my Love,
    And in my soule am free;
Angels alone that sore above,
    Injoy such Liberty.

RICHARD LOVELACE (1618-56/7/8)

'If thou must love me'

(Sonnets from the Portuguese, XIV)

If thou must love me, let it be for nought
Except for love's sake only. Do not say
'I love her for her smile – her look – her way
Of speaking gently, – for a trick of thought
That falls in well with mine, and certes brought
A sense of pleasant ease on such a day' –
For these things in themselves, Belovèd, may
Be changed, or change for thee, – and love, so wrought,
May be unwrought so. Neither love me for
Thine own dear pity's wiping my cheeks dry, –
A creature might forget to weep, who bore
Thy comfort long, and lose thy love thereby!
But love me for love's sake, that evermore
Thou may'st love on, through love's eternity.

ELIZABETH BARRETT BROWNING (1806-61)

9

'If ever two were one,
then surely we'

(ANNE BRADSTREET)

Wedding-Wind

The wind blew all my wedding-day,
And my wedding-night was the night of the high wind;
And a stable door was banging, again and again,
That he must go and shut it, leaving me
Stupid in candlelight, hearing rain,
Seeing my face in the twisted candlestick,
Yet seeing nothing. When he came back
He said the horses were restless, and I was sad
That any man or beast that night should lack
The happiness I had.

               Now in the day
All's ravelled under the sun by the wind's blowing.
He has gone to look at the floods, and I
Carry a chipped pail to the chicken-run,
Set it down, and stare. All is the wind
Hunting through clouds and forests, thrashing
My apron and the hanging cloths on the line.
Can it be borne, this bodying-forth by wind
Of joy my actions turn on, like a thread
Carrying beads? Shall I be let to sleep
Now this perpetual morning shares my bed?
Can even death dry up
These new delighted lakes, conclude
Our kneeling as cattle by all-generous waters?

PHILIP LARKIN (1922-85)

Wedding

From time to time our love is like a sail
and when the sail begins to alternate
from tack to tack, it's like a swallowtail
and when the swallow flies it's like a coat;

166

and if the coat is yours, it has a tear
like a wide mouth and when the mouth begins
to draw the wind, it's like a trumpeter
and when the trumpet blows, it blows like millions...
and this, my love, when millions come and go
beyond the need of us, is like a trick;
and when the trick begins, it's like a toe
tiptoeing on a rope, which is like luck;
and when the luck begins, it's like a wedding,
which is like love, which is like everything.

ALICE OSWALD (b. 1966)

'By this he knew she wept with waking eyes'
(Modern Love, 1)

By this he knew she wept with waking eyes:
That, at his hand's light quiver by her head,
The strange low sobs that shook their common bed,
Were called into her with a sharp surprise,
And strangled mute, like little gaping snakes,
Dreadfully venomous to him. She lay
Stone-still, and the long darkness flowed away
With muffled pulses. Then, as midnight makes
Her giant heart of Memory and Tears
Drink the pale drug of silence, and so beat
Sleep's heavy measure, they from head to feet
Were moveless, looking through their dead black years,
By vain regret scrawled over the blank wall.
Like sculptured effigies they might be seen
Upon their marriage-tomb, the sword between;
Each wishing for the sword that severs all.

GEORGE MEREDITH (1828-1909)

An Epitaph upon Husband and Wife who died and were buried together

To these whom death again did wed
This grave's the second marriage-bed.
For though the hand of Fate could force
'Twixt soul and body a divorce,
It could not sever man and wife,
Because they both lived but one life.
Peace, good reader, do not weep;
Peace, the lovers are asleep.
They, sweet turtles, folded lie
In the last knot that love could tie.
Let them sleep, let them sleep on,
Till the stormy night be gone,
And the eternal morrow dawn;
Then the curtains will be drawn,
And they wake into a light
Whose day shall never die in night.

RICHARD CRASHAW (1612/3-49)

Marriage I Think

Marriage I think
For women
Is the best of opiates.
It kills the thoughts
That think about the thoughts,
It is the best of opiates.
So said Maria.
But too long in solitude she'd dwelt,
And too long her thoughts had felt
Their strength. So when the man drew near,
Out popped her thoughts and covered him with fear.
Poor Maria!

Better that she had kept her thoughts on a chain,
For now she's alone again and all in pain;
She sighs for the man that went and the thoughts that stay
To trouble her dreams by night and her dreams by day.

STEVIE SMITH (1902-71)

To Wed or Not to Wed

To wed, or not to wed: that is the question:
Whether 'tis nobler in the mind to suffer
The fret and loneliness of spinsterhood
Or to take arms against the single state
And by marrying, end it? To wed; to match,
No more; yet by this match to say we end
The heartache and the thousand natural shocks
That flesh is heir to; 'tis a consummation
Devoutly to be wish'd. To wed, to match;
To match, perchance mismatch: aye, there's the rub;
For in that match what dread mishaps may come,
When we have shuffled off this single state
For wedded bliss: there's the respect
That makes singleness of so long life,
For who'd forgo the joys of wife and mother,
The pleasures of devotion, of sacrifice and love
The blessings of a home and all home means,
The restful sympathy of soul to soul,
The loved ones circling round at eventide
When she herself might gain all these
With a marriage vow? Who would fardels bear
To pine and sigh under a single life
But that the dread of something after marriage,
That undiscovered nature, from whose ways
One scarce can sever, puzzles the will,
And makes us rather cling to single bliss
Than barter that we know for things unsure?

Thus dreadful doubt makes cowards of us all
And thus the native hue of resolution
Is sicklied o'er with the pale cast of thought,
And matrimonial rites, and wedded life
With this regard their currents turn awry
And lose the name of action.

(With apologies to Shakespeare)

UNA MARSON (1905-65)

An Answer to another perswading a Lady to Marriage

Forbear bold Youth, all's Heaven here,
    And what you do aver,
To others Courtship may appear,
    'Tis Sacriledge to her.

She is publick Deity,
    And were't not very odd
She should depose her self to be
    A petty Houshold God?

First make the Sun in private shine,
    And bid the World adieu,
That so he may his beams confine
    In complement to you.

But if of that you do despair,
    Think how you did amiss,
To strive to fix her beams which are
    More bright and large than his.

KATHERINE PHILIPS (1631-64)

Sonnet

Oh, oh, you will be sorry for that word!
Give back my book and take my kiss instead.
Was it my enemy or my friend I heard,
'What a big book for such a little head!'
Come, I will show you now my newest hat,
And you may watch me purse my mouth and prink!
Oh, I shall love you still, and all of that.
I never again shall tell you what I think.
I shall be sweet and crafty, soft and sly;
You will not catch me reading any more:
I shall be called a wife to pattern by;
And some day when you knock and push the door,
Some sane day, not too bright and not too stormy,
I shall be gone, and you may whistle for me.

EDNA ST VINCENT MILLAY (1892-1950)

For a Wedding
(Camilla and Kieran 9/8/94)

Cousin, I think the shape of a marriage
is like the shelves my parents have carried
through Scotland to London, three houses;

is not distinguished, fine, French-polished,
but plywood and tatty, made
in the first place for children to batter,

still carrying markings in green felt-tip,
but always, where there are books
and a landing, managing to fit;

that marriage has lumps like
their button-backed sofa, constantly,
shortly, about to be stuffed;

and that love grows fat
as their squinting cat, swelling
round as a loaf from her basket.

I wish you years that shape, that form,
and a pond in a Sunday, urban garden;
where you'll see your joined reflection tremble,

stand and watch the waterboatmen
skate with ease across the surface tension.

KATE CLANCHY (*b.* 1965)

To My Dear and Loving Husband

If ever two were one, then surely we.
If ever man were loved by wife, then thee.
If ever wife was happy in a man,
Compare with me, ye women, if you can.
I prize thy love more than whole mines of gold,
Or all the riches that the east doth hold.
My love is such that rivers cannot quench,
Nor ought but love from thee give recompence.
Thy love is such I can no way repay;
The heavens reward thee manifold I pray.
Then while we live, in love let's so persever,
Then when we live no more, we may live ever.

ANNE BRADSTREET (1612?-72)

A Ditty

My true-love hath my heart, and I have his,
By just exchange one to the other given:
I hold his dear, and mine he cannot miss,
There never was a better bargain driven:
My true-love hath my heart, and I have his.

His heart in me keeps him and me in one,
My heart in him his thoughts and senses guides:
He loves my heart, for once it was his own,
I cherish his because in me it bides:
My true-love hath my heart, and I have his.

SIR PHILIP SIDNEY (1554-86)

Love Song

How might I keep my soul from touching yours?
How should I try to set it free,
to lift it higher? How willingly
I'd hide it in some foreign, distant place,
in darkness, silence; among desolate things
that would not answer when your spirit sings.

All that can touch on us, myself and you,
draws us together as a fiddler's bow
playing upon two strings can draw one sound:
upon what instrument have we been strung?
And what musician holds us in his hand?
How sweet the song!

RAINER MARIA RILKE (1875-1926)
translated from the German by Stephen Cohn

The Quarrel

Suddenly, after the quarrel, while we waited,
Disheartened, silent, with downcast looks, nor stirred
Eyelid nor finger, hopeless both, yet hoping
Against all hope to unsay the sundering word:

While all the room's stillness deepened, deepened about us
And each of us crept his thought's way to discover
How, with as little sound as the fall of a leaf,
The shadow had fallen, and lover quarreled with lover;

And while, in the quiet, I marveled – alas, alas –
At your deep beauty, your tragic beauty, torn
As the pale flower is torn by the wanton sparrow –
This beauty, pitied and loved, and now forsworn;

It was then, when the instant darkened to its darkest, –
When faith was lost with hope, and the rain conspired
To strike its gray arpeggios against our heartstrings, –
When love no longer dared, and scarcely desired:

It was then that suddenly, in the neighbor's room,
The music started: that brave quartette of strings
Breaking out of the stillness, as out of our stillness,
Like the indomitable heart of life that sings

When all is lost; and startled from our sorrow,
Tranced from our grief by that diviner grief,
We raised remembering eyes, each looked at other,
Blinded with tears of joy; and another leaf

Fell silently as that first; and in the instant
The shadow had gone, our quarrel became absurd;
And we rose, to the angelic voices of the music,
And I touched your hand, and we kissed, without a word.

CONRAD AIKEN (1889-1973)

Love Comes Quietly

Love comes quietly,
finally, drops
about me, on me,
in the old ways.

What did I know
thinking myself
able to go
alone all the way.

ROBERT CREELEY (*b.* 1926)

True Love

In the middle of the night, when we get up
after making love, we look at each other
in total friendship, we know so fully
what the other has been doing. Bound to each other like
soldiers coming out of a battle,
bound with the tie of the birth-room, we
wander down the hall to the bathroom, I can
hardly walk, we weave through the dark
soft air, I know where you are
with my eyes closed, we are bound to each other with the
huge invisible threads of sex, though our
sexes themselves are muted, dark and
exhausted and delicately crushed, the whole
body is a sex – surely this
is the most blessed time of life,
the children deep asleep in their beds like a
vein of coal and a vein of gold
not discovered yet. I sit on the
toilet in the dark, you are somewhere in the room, I

open the window and the snow has fallen in a
deep drift against the pane, I
look up into it, a
world of cold crystals, silent and
glistening so I call out to you and you
come and hold my hand and I say
I cannot see beyond it! I cannot see beyond it!

SHARON OLDS (*b.* 1942)

We Took the Storms to Bed

We took the storms to bed at night
When first we loved. A spark
Sprang outward from our loins to light
Like genesis the dark.

On other things our minds were bent,
We did not hear the Word,
But locked like Sarah in her tent
The listening belly heard.

And though we wept, she laughed aloud
And fattened on her mirth:
As strange as creatures from a cloud
Our children walk the earth.

DAVID CAMPBELL (1915-79)

Happy Together

Now they are sleeping, or almost, we're downstairs
dancing in the front room, staunching the flow
of busy weekends by binding ourselves
to ourselves. We're happy together.
Our discussions have proved this, but now and again
it comes banging through the house, doors slammed
by a summer breeze with some ferocity.
Such grief. Is it possible where our concerns
are focused on food and sleep? Digging the garden
we're telling the children about the way
things grow, knowing it's more than soil
and water and a good dose of sun,
but also the vision of losing the lot.

JONATHAN DAVIDSON (*b.* 1964)

Natural History
(A letter to Katherine, from the King Edward Hotel, Toronto)

The spider, dropping down from twig,
Unwinds a thread of her devising:
A thin, premeditated rig
To use in rising.

And all the journey down through space,
In cool descent and loyal-hearted,
She builds a ladder to the place
From which she started.

Thus I, gone forth, as spiders do,
In spider's web a truth discerning,
Attach one silken strand to you
For my returning.

E.B. WHITE (1899-1995)

From Cheshire

(for Anna)

Come home safe: I think of you driving
  Over the Runcorn Bridge in our senile car,
Its toothless ratchets, arthritic pistons conniving
  To take me away from wherever you are.

Its steering like that old prostitute working a living
  On Huskisson Street outside our door:
Its raggedy brake shoes thin as the wind, giving
  Nothing but ice to your foot on the floor.

Please come home: I think of you leaving
  For ever, coming from Cheshire, only the snow
And the night and the endless black road, no retrieving
  Of you: without me, wherever I go.

KIT WRIGHT (*b.* 1944)

The Heart's Wild Geese

Heart must always come again to home,
Like the wild geese who wheel their way through time
Back to the timeless pool and homely sedge.
They who went questing, screaming to the edge
Of man's small world, over the edge some say,
Have seen the iceberg's glory, seen the way
The coloured sun hangs curtains in the sky,
The barren coves where ancient whales still lie
Covered with barnacles as old as Spain,
Living the glorious bloody days again
When dragon-prowed boats first thrust through their dream.

All this the wild geese see, and their strange scream
Sounds back along the centuries. They know
Where palaces lie buried in the snow;
In passing, their sharp eyes have often snatched
At coral-courts, where rituals unwatched
By any other eye save gull's are kept
By weed-green seamen who have safely slept
Three hundred years a thousand leagues from home.
And after all these marvels still they come,
The feathered faithful, landing on the mere
As heart returns to home, year upon year.

HENRY TREECE (1911-66)

Anne Hathaway

'Item I gyve unto my wief my second best bed...'
(from Shakespeare's will)

The bed we loved in was a spinning world
of forests, castles, torchlight, clifftops, seas
where he would dive for pearls. My lover's words
were shooting stars which fell to earth as kisses
on these lips; my body now a softer rhyme
to his, now echo, assonance; his touch
a verb dancing in the centre of a noun.
Some nights, I dreamed he'd written me, the bed
a page beneath his writer's hands. Romance
and drama played by touch, by scent, by taste.
In the other bed, the best, our guests dozed on,
dribbling their prose. My living laughing love –
I hold him in the casket of my widow's head
as he held me upon that next best bed.

CAROL ANN DUFFY (*b*. 1955)

Home

Has canary-yellow curtains, so expensive
At certain times they become unaffordable,
Cost too much patience. A cartoon voice:

'I'm leaving, Elmer.' That's home also, sometimes;
The Eden a person can't go back to. Still...
If you don't leave it, it's only a world;

If you never return, just a place like any other.
Home isn't in the *Blue Guide*, the A–Z
I only need for those ten thousand streets

Not one of which has Alice Wales in it.
At home you bolt on the new pine headboard,
Crying. You build from your tears

A hydroponicum; bitter-sweet nutrition
Becomes the address we ripen in like fruit
No one thought would grow here. Home

Is where we hang up our clothes and surnames
Without thought. Home is the instruction: dream home.
An architecture of faint clicks, and smells that haven't yet quite.

We grow old in it. Like children, it keeps us young,
Every evening being twenty-one again
With the key in the door, coming back from the library

You're shouting upstairs to me, telling me what you are
In the simplest of words, that I want you to go on repeating
Like a call-sign. You are shouting, 'I'm home.'

ROBERT CRAWFORD (b. 1959)

Passing Remark

In scenery I like flat country.
In life I don't like much to happen.

In personalities I like mild colorless people.
And in colors I prefer gray and brown.

My wife, a vivid girl from the mountains,
says, 'Then why did you choose me?'

Mildly I lower my brown eyes –
there are so many things admirable people do not understand.

WILLIAM STAFFORD (1914-93)

The Underground

There we were in the vaulted tunnel running,
You in your going-away coat speeding ahead
And me, me then like a fleet god gaining
Upon you before you turned to a reed

Or some new white flower japped with crimson
As the coat flapped wild and button after button
Sprang off and fell in a trail
Between the Underground and the Albert Hall.

Honeymooning, mooning aground, late for the Proms,
Our echoes die in that corridor and now
I come as Hansel came on the moonlit stones
Retracing the path back, lifting the buttons

To end up in a draughty lamplit station
After the trains have gone, the wet track
Bared and tensed as I am, all attention
For your step following and damned if I look back.

SEAMUS HEANEY (*b.* 1939)

Underworld

What if you have swallowed me,
swallowed six pomegranate seeds
and split your life? Must I let you go
down alone into each night as winter,
the path behind you freezing over?

Will I learn not to cry after,
to lie still on the ice, to know this is
not for ever, that the sky will crack
and I will fall through and wake with you
in something of summer?

LAVINIA GREENLAW (*b.* 1962)

The Owl and the Pussy-Cat

The Owl and the Pussy-Cat went to sea
   In a beautiful pea-green boat.
They took some honey, and plenty of money
   Wrapped up in a five-pound note.
The Owl looked up to the stars above,
   And sang to a small guitar,
'O lovely Pussy! O Pussy, my love,
What a beautiful Pussy you are,
     You are,
     You are!
What a beautiful Pussy you are!'

Pussy said to the Owl, 'You elegant fowl!
   How charmingly sweet you sing!
O let us be married! too long we have tarried:
   But what shall we do for a ring?'
They sailed away, for a year and a day,
   To the land where the Bong-Tree grows,

And there in a wood a Piggy-wig stood,
With a ring at the end of his nose,
 His nose,
 His nose!
With a ring at the end of his nose.

'Dear Pig, are you willing to sell for one shilling
 Your ring?' Said the Piggy, 'I will.'
So they took it away, and were married next day
 By the Turkey who lives on the hill.
They dinèd on mince, and slices of quince,
 Which they ate with a runcible spoon;
And hand in hand, on the edge of the sand
 They danced by the light of the moon,
  The moon,
  The moon,
They danced by the light of the moon.

EDWARD LEAR (1812-88)

Ode

'To depict a (bicycle), you must first come to love (it).'
ALEKSANDR BLOK

I swear by every rule in the bicycle
owner's manual

that I love you, I, who have repeatedly,
painstakingly,

with accompanying declaration of despair,
tried to repair

you, to patch things up,
to maintain a workable relationship.

I have spent sleepless nights
in pondering your parts – those private

and those that all who walk the street
may look at –

wondering what makes you tick
over smoothly, or squeak.

O my trusty steed,
my rusty three-speed,

I would feed you the best oats
if oats

were applicable.
Only linseed oil

will do
to nourish you.

I want
so much to paint

you,
midnight blue

mudgutter black
and standing as you do, ironic

at the rail
provided by the Council –

beautiful
the sun caught in your back wheel –

or at home in the hall, remarkable
among other bicycles,

your handlebars erect.
Allow me to depict

you thus. And though I can't do justice
to your true opinion of the surface

of the road –
put into words

the nice distinctions that you make
among the different sorts of tarmac –

still I'd like to set the record of our travels straight.
I'd have you know that

not with three-in-one
but with my own

heart's
spittle I anoint your moving parts.

GILLIAN ALLNUTT (*b.* 1949)

Bike

You, who have borne three sons
of mine, still bear my weight
routinely, transporting me.

An odd pair: your classic spare
lines – elbows, bony frame –
and me, bearlike, cumbersome,

nosing tangled coils of air
you cut through with your pure
purposeful geometry.

With you it's feet off the ground,
a feat passing unremarked
though in full public view.

Keeping each other's balance.
Our talk slow recurrent clicks,
companionable creaks.

Through you I've come to know
winds inside out and raw
weather ignored before;

and nuances of slopes,
the moving earth, green tracks
for blackberries and sloes

for gin, for jam: the tug
and tang of fruit pulling me
clear of the wheel of myself.

MICHAEL LASKEY (*b*. 1944)

Long Finish

Ten years since we were married, since we stood
under a chuppah of pine boughs
in the middle of a little pinewood
and exchanged our wedding vows.
Save me, good thou,
a piece of marchpane, while I fill your glass with Simi
Chardonnay as high as decency allows,
and then some.

Bear with me now as I myself must bear
the scrutiny of a bottle of wine
that boasts of hints of plum and pear,
its muscadine
tempered by an oak backbone. I myself have designs
on the willow-boss
of your breast, on all your waist confines
between longing and loss.

The wonder is that we somehow have withstood
the soars and slumps in the Dow
of ten years of marriage and parenthood,
its summits and its sloughs –
that we've somehow
managed to withstand an almond-blossomy
five years of bitter rapture, five of blissful rows
(and then some,

if we count the one or two to spare
when we've been firmly on cloud nine).
Even now, as you turn away from me with your one bare
shoulder, the veer of your neckline,
I glimpse the all-but-cleared-up eczema patch on your spine
and it brings to mind not the Schloss
that stands, transitory, tra la, Triestine,
between longing and loss

but a crude
hip-trench in a field, covered with pine boughs,
in which two men in masks and hoods
who have themselves taken vows
wait for a farmer to break a bale for his cows
before opening fire with semi-
automatics, cutting him off slightly above the eyebrows,
and then some.

It brings to mind another, driving out to care
for six white-faced kine
finishing on heather and mountain air,
another who'll shortly divine
the precise whereabouts of a landmine
on the road between Beragh and Sixmilecross,
who'll shortly know what it is to have breasted the line
between longing and loss.

Such forbearance in the face of vicissitude
also brings to mind the little 'there, there's and 'now, now's
of two sisters whose sleeves are imbued
with the constant douse and souse
of salt-water through their salt-house
in *Matsukaze* (or 'Pining Wind'), by Zeami,
the salt-house through which the wind soughs and soughs,
and then some

of the wind's little 'now, now's and 'there, there's
seem to intertwine
with those of Pining Wind and Autumn Rain, who must forbear
the dolor of their lives of boiling down brine.
For the double meaning of 'pine'
is much the same in Japanese as English, coming across
both in the sense of 'tree' and the sense we assign
between 'longing' and 'loss'

as when the ghost of Yukihira, the poet-courtier who wooed
both sisters, appears as a ghostly pine, pining among pine boughs.
Barely have Autumn Rain and Pining Wind renewed
their vows
than you turn back towards me and your blouse,
while it covers the all-but-cleared-up patch of eczema,
falls as low as decency allows,
and then some.

Princess of Accutane, let's no more try to refine
the pure drop from the dross
than distinguish, good thou, between mine and thine,
between longing and loss,
but rouse
ourselves each dawn, here on the shore at Suma,
with such force and fervor as spouses may yet espouse,
and then some.

PAUL MULDOON (*b.* 1952)

To My Wife at Midnight

1

Are you to say goodnight
And turn away under
The blanket of your delight?

Are you to let me go
Alone to sleep beside you
Into the drifting snow?

Where we each reach,
Sleeping alone together,
Nobody can touch.

Is the cat's window open?
Shall I turn into your back?
And what is to happen?

What is to happen to us
And what is to happen to each
Of us asleep in our places?

2

I mean us both going
Into sleep at our ages
To sleep and get our fairing.

They have all gone home.
Night beasts are coming out.
The black wood of Madron

Is just waking up.
I hear the rain outside
To help me to go to sleep.

Nessie, don't let my soul
Skip and miss a beat
And cause me to fall.

3

Are you asleep I say
Into the back of your neck
For you not to hear me.

Are you asleep? I hear
Your heart under the pillow
Saying my dear my dear

My dear for all it's worth.
Where is the dun's moor
Which began your breath?

4

Ness, to tell you the truth
I am drifting away
Down to fish for the saithe.

Is the cat's window open?
The weather is on my shoulder
And I am drifting down

Into O can you hear me
Among your Dunsmuir Clan?
Are you coming out to play?

5

Did I behave badly
On the field at Culloden?
I lie sore-wounded now

By all activities, and
The terrible acts of my time
Are only a distant sound.

With responsibility
I am drifting off
Breathing regularly

Into my younger days
To play the games of Greenock
Beside the sugar-house quays.

6

Nessie Dunsmuir, I say
Wheesht wheesht to myself
To help me now to go

Under into somewhere
In the redcoat rain.
Buckle me for the war.

Are you to say goodnight
And kiss me and fasten
My drowsy armour tight?

My dear camp-follower,
Hap the blanket round me
And tuck in a flower.

Maybe from my sleep
In the stoure at Culloden
I'll see you here asleep

In your lonely place.

W.S. GRAHAM (1918-86)

The Hug

It was your birthday, we had drunk and dined
   Half of the night with our old friend
     Who'd showed us in the end
   To a bed I reached in one drunk stride.
     Already I lay snug,
And drowsy with the wine dozed on one side.

I dozed, I slept. My sleep broke on a hug,
     Suddenly, from behind,
In which the full lengths of our bodies pressed:
     Your instep to my heel,
   My shoulder-blades against your chest.

It was not sex, but I could feel
The whole strength of your body set,
      Or braced, to mine,
    And locking me to you
As if we were still twenty-two
When our grand passion had not yet
      Become familial.
My quick sleep had deleted all
Of intervening time and place.
      I only knew
The stay of your secure firm dry embrace.

THOM GUNN (*b.* 1929)

Kissing

The young are walking on the riverbank,
arms around each other's waists and shoulders,
pretending to be looking at the waterlilies
and what might be a nest of some kind, over
there, which two who are clamped together
mouth to mouth have forgotten about.
The others, making courteous detours
around them, talk, stop talking, kiss.
They can see no one older than themselves.
It's their river. They've got all day.

Seeing's not everything. At this very
moment the middle-aged are kissing
in the backs of taxis, on the way
to airports and stations. Their mouths and tongues
are soft and powerful and as moist as ever.
Their hands are not inside each other's clothes
(because of the driver) but locked so tightly
together that it hurts: it may leave marks
on their not of course youthful skin, which they won't
notice. They too may have futures.

FLEUR ADCOCK (*b.* 1934)

Elizabeth

(from 'Summer')

An unaccustomed ripeness in the wood;
move but an inch and moldy splinters fall
in sawdust from the walls' aluminum-paint,
once loud and fresh, now aged to weathered wood.
Squalls of the seagull's exaggerated outcry
dim out in the fog... *Pace, pace.* All day our words
were rusty fish-hooks – wormwood... Dear Heart's-Ease,
we rest from all discussion, drinking, smoking,
pills for high blood, three pairs of glasses – soaking
in the sweat of our hard-earned supremacy,
offering a child our leathery love. We're fifty,
and free! Young, tottering on the dizzying brink
of discretion once, you wanted nothing,
but to be old, do nothing, type and think.

ROBERT LOWELL (1917-77)

Snap

In this light, your lips open
like a red flower; a sparkler in your hair.
Strange things always happen for our love.
We watch deer dance towards us in red light
far above the city. We go to speak the same word.

In this light, the graveyard is haunting, beautiful.
The gold trees guard the stones like faithful dogs.
We start to say we wouldn't mind being buried here:
till the barn owl sings its one note
on the gloved hand of an Irish man.

JACKIE KAY (b. 1961)

Old Age

Later, when I am feeble-minded
with lapdog and frightskin
I'll keep a bottle warm
against me and talk
to you in my sleep.
If you can understand now
what I'm going to mean then
crackling withered stem that I'll be
I will not feel so broken off
more like a blown-out dandelion.
You hear me babble?
There go my little parachutes.

JUDITH HERZBERG (*b.* 1934)
translated from the Dutch by the author

Talking in Bed

Talking in bed ought to be easiest,
Lying together there goes back so far,
An emblem of two people being honest.

Yet more and more time passes silently.
Outside, the wind's incomplete unrest
Builds and disperses clouds about the sky,

And dark towns heap up on the horizon.
None of this cares for us. Nothing shows why
At this unique distance from isolation

It becomes still more difficult to find
Words at once true and kind,
Or not untrue and not unkind.

PHILIP LARKIN (1922-85)

Conversation

For forty years they had lived with each other
and the language was growing harder and harder to understand
at first they had known a few words
later on they made do with nods:
bed and food.
For forty years they had coped with the day-to-day.
Their faces grew calmer, like stones,
But sometimes a chance interpreter appeared:
a cat, an unusual sunset
they would listen with an air of unease
try to answer
                  they were already speechless.

SOLVEIG VON SCHOULTZ (1907-96)
translated from Finland Swedish by David McDuff

'When you are old'
(Sonnets for Helen, II, 42)

When you are old, and sitting, candle-lit,
Close to the fire, teasing and spinning wool,
You'll sing my lines and, wondering, admit,
'Ronsard praised me, when I was beautiful.'

Then what young servant of that future house,
To hear of you and Ronsard, will not raise
Her drooping head from work, start from her drowse
And bless your name for that immortal praise.

I shall be fleshless, ghostly under earth,
Among the lovers' shades at last at rest,
You an old woman bent beside the hearth
Regretting that I loved and you said Nay.

    Live now, don't wait, don't think tomorrow's best:
Gather the roses of this life today.

PIERRE DE RONSARD (1524-85)
translated from the French by Alistair Elliot

When You Are Old

When you are old and grey and full of sleep,
And nodding by the fire, take down this book,
And slowly read, and dream of the soft look
Your eyes had once, and of their shadows deep;

How many loved your moments of glad grace,
And loved your beauty with love false or true,
But one man loved the pilgrim soul in you,
And loved the sorrows of your changing face;

And bending down beside the glowing bars,
Murmur, a little sadly, how Love fled
And paced upon the mountains overhead
And hid his face amid a crowd of stars.

W.B. YEATS (1865-1939)

Stella's Birthday
[1718/9]

Stella this day is thirty-four,
(We shan't dispute a year or more)
However Stella, be not troubled,
Although thy size and years are doubled,
Since first I saw thee at sixteen
The brightest virgin of the green,
So little is thy form declin'd;
Made up so largely in thy mind.

Oh, would it please the gods, to split
Thy beauty, size, and years, and wit,
No age could furnish out a pair
Of nymphs so graceful, wise, and fair
With half the lustre of your eyes,
With half your wit, your years, and size.

And then, before it grew too late,
How should I beg of gentle Fate,
(That either nymph might have her swain)
To split my worship too in twain.

JONATHAN SWIFT (1667-1745)

To Dr Swift on his Birthday,
30th November 1721

St Patrick's Dean, your country's pride,
My early and my only guide,
You taught how I might youth prolong,
By knowing what was right and wrong;
How from my heart to bring supplies
Of lustre to my fading eyes;
How soon a beauteous mind repairs
The loss of changed or falling hairs;
How wit and virtue from within
Send out a smoothness o'er the skin;
Your lectures could my fancy fix,
And I can please at thirty-six.
The sight of Chloe at fifteen,
Coquetting, gives me not the spleen;
The idol now of every fool
Till time shall make their passions cool;
Then tumbling down Time's steepy hill,
While Stella holds her station still.

ESTHER JOHNSON (1681 1723)

I Knew a Woman

I knew a woman, lovely in her bones,
When small birds sighed, she would sigh back at them;
Ah, when she moved, she moved more ways than one:
The shapes a bright container can contain!
Of her choice virtues only gods should speak,
Or English poets who grew up on Greek
(I'd have them sing in chorus, cheek to cheek).

How well her wishes went! She stroked my chin,
She taught me Turn, and Counter-turn, and Stand;
She taught me Touch, that undulant white skin;
I nibbled meekly from her proffered hand;
She was the sickle; I, poor I, the rake,
Coming behind her for her pretty sake
(But what prodigious mowing we did make).

Love likes a gander, and adores a goose:
Her full lips pursed, the errant note to seize;
She played it quick, she played it light and loose;
My eyes, they dazzled at her flowing knees;
Her several parts could keep a pure repose,
Or one hip quiver with a mobile nose
(She moved in circles, and those circles moved).

Let seed be grass, and grass turn into hay:
I'm martyr to a motion not my own;
What's freedom for? To know eternity.
I swear she cast a shadow white as stone.
But who would count eternity in days?
These old bones live to learn her wanton ways:
(I measure time by how a body sways).

THEODORE ROETHKE (1908-63)

198

The Table

Remember that table we used to want?
That we agreed should be plain, serviceable wood,
with drop leaves, to complete our tiny room.

Something to which baby-chairs could be yoked,
that might expand, in time, for supper-parties,
for renewed experiments with the spirit lamp.

Across which, over the wine and profiteroles,
we could tell each other stories: how I was thrown
off a buckrake under the back wheel of the tractor;

while you, a girl in Ontario, stuck your barrette
in a socket and were saved from electrocution
by its rubber band. You'd gloss *barrette* as hair-slide.

And we'd agree these were simultaneous events,
so we might chuckle once more at the providence
of coming together, to increase and multiply,

here, around a table we'd hunted down in New Cross,
having perambulated your bump (the twin-tub!)
through loft upon loft of displaced furniture.

We never gave up on that table, you know,
not officially. And I've kept an eye out for it,
scanning from habit the small ads and auction lists.

Would you believe me now if I telephoned
to say I'd found one? Nothing fancy or antique,
but an honest specimen of forties joinery.

It would require work. That marbled green veneer
would have to go, along with several nicks
and gouges, obscure stains, other people's memories.

Sure – a lot of work. But you can still see
somewhere inside it the original shining deal,
the plain altar still fit for household ceremonies.

MAURICE RIORDAN (*b.* 1953)

On the Table

I would like to make it clear that I have bought
this tablecloth with its simple repeating pattern
of dark purple blooms not named by any botanist
because it reminds me of that printed dress you had
the summer we met – a dress you have always said
I never told you I liked. Well I did, you know. I did.
I liked it a lot, whether you were inside it or not.

How did it slip so quietly out of our life?
I hate – I really hate – to think of some other bum
swinging those heavy flower-heads left to right.
I hate even more to think of it mouldering on a tip
or torn to shreds – a piece here wiping a dipstick,
a piece there tied round a crack in a lead pipe.

It's all a long time ago now, darling, a long time,
but tonight just like our first night here I am
with my head light in my hands and my glass full,
staring at the big drowsy petals until they start to swim,
loving them but wishing to lift them aside, unbutton them,
tear them, even, if that's what it takes to get through
to the beautiful, moon-white, warm, wanting skin of you.

ANDREW MOTION (*b.* 1952)

The Knife

You brought it with you to the marriage
I think, already in your kitchen drawer
in Savernake Road when we first
pooled our possessions. A perfectly
ordinary kitchen knife: the two
rivets through the dark stained wood
of the handle still holding the blade

firmly after twenty years. Signs
of wear though, as you'd expect: the tip
broken off – used as a lever once
too often – a nick in the edge
and the brown handle mottled, streaked
unevenly where the wood dye's leached.
I like it sharp: gritting my teeth
I grind it between steel wheels
now and again, scare my thumb.
It fits my fist, loves stringing beans,
slicing onions, tomatoes, courgettes.
Who'd have thought it would come to matter
so much to me, this small knife
you say now you're not sure was yours?

MICHAEL LASKEY (*b*. 1944)

Autumn Violets

Keep love for youth, and violets for the spring:
  Or if these bloom when worn-out autumn grieves,
  Let them lie hid in double shade of leaves,
Their own, and others dropped down withering;
For violets suit when home birds build and sing,
  Not when the outbound bird a passage cleaves;
  Not with dry stubble of mown harvest sheaves,
But when the green world buds to blossoming.
Keep violets for the spring, and love for youth,
  Love that should dwell with beauty, mirth, and hope:
    Or if a later sadder love be born,
  Let this not look for grace beyond its scope,
But give itself, nor plead for answering truth –
    A grateful Ruth tho' gleaning scanty corn.

CHRISTINA ROSSETTI (1830-94)

Black Violets

If I say 'black violets' our first night
is nearly dark enough to draw this daylight rain
to memory's nomadic glistening, and I can
be there again, carrying love
to love in that room where his last heart
gave over its invisible amber. It's true,
he's evergreen in me and I make green use of him
to love you all the way back through death
into life again. I bury us in him and dig
us out again until we are a moon
that has passed through a mountain in order
to climb the night sky with no voice, no mouth,
no bodily empire except this lonely passage
for which he lends goodly silence and
the distance by which a moon can rise.

In that pang of earth you cast into me
he stepped forward, accompanied us
a little way into the present, into the sweetness
of so much yet to be lived out in this retrieval
of my unretrievable heart.
If you were two men to me there
it was to make lucid a fresh outlasting.
The one in which yours are the lips, yours
the enfolding vastness, this black rushing
of tiny fragrant faces against our skin, the violets
we feed each other petal by velvet
petal to keep the night long enough
for this new-made heart to open us in blood-darkness
into its farthest chamber.

TESS GALLAGHER (*b.* 1943)

Rooms

I remember rooms that have had their part
  In the steady slowing down of the heart.
The room in Paris, the room at Geneva,
The little damp room with the seaweed smell,
And that ceaseless maddening sound of the tide –
  Rooms where for good or for ill – things died.
But there is the room where we (two) lie dead,
Though every morning we seem to wake and might just as well
                                   seem to sleep again
  As we shall somewhere in the other quieter, dustier bed
  Out there in the sun – in the rain.

CHARLOTTE MEW (1869-1928)

And You, Helen

And you, Helen, what should I give you?
So many things I would give you
Had I an infinite great store
Offered me and I stood before
To choose. I would give you youth,
All kinds of loveliness and truth,
A clear eye as good as mine,
Lands, waters, flowers, wine,
As many children as your heart
Might wish for, a far better art
Than mine can be, all you have lost
Upon the travelling waters tossed,
Or given to me. If I could choose
Freely in that great treasure-house
Anything from any shelf,
I would give you back yourself,
And power to discriminate
What you want and want it not too late,

Many fair days free from care
And heart to enjoy both foul and fair,
And myself, too, if I could find
Where it lay hidden and it proved kind.

EDWARD THOMAS (1878-1917)

Atlas

There is a kind of love called maintenance,
Which stores the WD40 and knows when to use it;

Which checks the insurance, and doesn't forget
The milkman; which remembers to plant bulbs;

Which answers letters; which knows the way
The money goes; which deals with dentists

And Road Fund Tax and meeting trains,
And postcards to the lonely; which upholds

The permanently ricketty elaborate
Structures of living; which is Atlas.

And maintenance is the sensible side of love,
Which knows what time and weather are doing
To my brickwork; insulates my faulty wiring;
Laughs at my dryrotten jokes; remembers
My need for gloss and grouting; which keeps
My suspect edifice upright in air,
As Atlas did the sky.

U.A. FANTHORPE (b. 1929)

10

'I am no good at love'

(NOEL COWARD)

Comment

Oh, life is a glorious cycle of song,
A medley of extemporanea;
And love is a thing that can never go wrong,
And I am Marie of Rumania.

DOROTHY PARKER (1893-1967)

A Learned Mistress

Tell him it's all a lie;
    I love him as much as my life;
He needn't be jealous of me –
    I love him and loathe his wife.

If he kill me through jealousy now
    His wife will perish of spite,
He'll die of grief for his wife –
    Three of us dead in a night.

All blessings from heaven to earth
    On the head of the woman I hate,
And the man I love as my life,
    Sudden death be his fate.

ISOBEL CAMPBELL (*c.* 1200)
translated from the Gaelic by Frank O'Connor

I've dissolved for you

I've dissolved for you, in that glass over there,
A handful of my burnt hair.
So there will be no singing, no eating,
So there will be no drinking, no sleeping.

So your youth will lose its freshness,
And your sugar will lose its sweetness.
So at night you'll be locked in strife
With your young wife.

As my golden tresses
Have turned to grey ashes,
So your young years will be quite
Turned to winter, white.

So your ear will go deaf, and blind your eye,
So like moss you will become dry,
So you will vanish like a sigh.

MARINA TSVETAYEVA (1892-1941)
translated from the Russian by David McDuff

Bitcherel

You ask what I think of your new acquisition;
and since we are now to be 'friends',
I'll strive to the full to cement my position
with honesty. Dear – it depends.

It depends upon taste, which must not be disputed;
for which of us *does* understand
why some like their furnishings pallid and muted,
their cookery wholesome, but bland?

There isn't a *law* that a face should have features,
it's just that they generally *do*;
God couldn't give colour to *all* of his creatures,
and only gave wit to a few;

I'm sure she has qualities, much underrated,
that compensate amply for this,
along with a charm that is so understated
it's easy for people to miss.

And if there are some who choose clothing to flatter
what beauties they think they possess,
when what's underneath has no shape, does it matter
if there is no shape to the dress?

It's not that I think she is *boring*, precisely,
that isn't the word I would choose;
I know there are men who like girls who talk nicely
and always wear sensible shoes.

It's not that I think she is vapid and silly;
it's not that her voice makes me wince;
but – chilli con carne without any chilli
is only a plateful of mince...

ELEANOR BROWN (*b.* 1969)

from The Wife of Bath's Tale

And whan the knyght saugh verraily al this,
That she so fair was, and so yong there-to,
For joye he hente hir in his armes two,
His herte bathed in a bath of blisse.
A thousand tyme a-newe he gan hir kisse,
And she obeyed hym in every thing
That myghte doon hym plesance or likyng.
    And thus they live unto hir lyves ende
In parfit joye; and Jhesu Crist us sende
Housbondes meeke, yonge, and fressh a-bedde,
And grace t'overbyde hem that we wedde;
And eek I praye Jhesu shorte hir lyves
That wol nat be governed by hir wyves;
And olde and angry nygardes of dispence,
God sende hem soone verray pestilence!

GEOFFREY CHAUCER (c.1343-1400)

The Folk I Love

I do hate the folk I love,
They hurt so.
Their least word and act may be
Source of woe.

'Won't you come to tea with me?'
'Not today.
I'm so tired, I've been to church.'
Such folk say.

All the dreary afternoon
I must clutch
At the strength to love like them,
Not too much.

LESBIA HARFORD (1881-1927)

Unsuitable Shoes

Sheep are the voices of the damned,
calling out to you as you stumble along,
demanding something you can't give
in this flimsy dress, these crazy shoes.

You're following him along a path
edged with the soft bodies of sheep.
It wasn't what you expected tonight
or what you told yourself was possible.

There is the slightest curve of moon,
the sighing of wind through gorse
still yellow in the half-light, the day's end,
when you are struggling over dried earth.

He slows, takes your hand across the stream,
an owl cries out, searching for voles,
your breath hurts in your chest, a fox slips
away knowing you are too close for comfort.

Red shoes covered in dust, fine leather
holding your feet like ballet pumps
but you're not dancing, only keeping up
while he takes you walking on the mountain.

It was never going to happen again,
you promised yourself after the last time.
This is the last time you said, wrote those
words on the inside of cigarette packets.

You got into the car just the same,
fastened your seat belt quick and tight,
not meaning to go this far, to jump out
lightly, skipping through the wide gate.

How you pretend, how you stay silent
when your feet hurt and the sheep's voices
remind you of where you should be, not here,
not ruining your pretty little shoes.

ALICIA STUBBERSFIELD (*b.* 1952)

'Sigh no more, Ladies'
(Much Ado About Nothing, II, 3)

Sigh no more, ladies, sigh no more!
  Men were deceivers ever,
One foot in sea, and one on shore;
  To one thing constant never.
    Then sigh not so,
    But let them go,
  And be you blithe and bonny,
Converting all your sounds of woe
  Into Hey nonny, nonny.

Sing no more ditties, sing no moe,
  Of dumps so dull and heavy!
The fraud of men was ever so,
  Since summer first was leavy.
    Then sigh not so,
    But let them go,
  And be you blithe and bonny,
Converting all your sounds of woe
  Into Hey nonny, nonny.

WILLIAM SHAKESPEARE (1564 1616)

from A Shropshire Lad
(XIII)

When I was one-and-twenty
  I heard a wise man say,
'Give crowns and pounds and guineas
  But not your heart away;
Give pearls away and rubies
  But keep your fancy free.'
But I was one-and-twenty,
  No use to talk to me.

When I was one-and-twenty
    I heard him say again,
'The heart out of the bosom
    Was never given in vain;
'Tis paid with sighs a plenty
    And sold for endless rue.'
And I am two-and-twenty,
    And oh, 'tis true, 'tis true.

A.E. HOUSMAN (1859-1936)

The Pity of Love

A pity beyond all telling
Is hid in the heart of love:
The folk who are buying and selling,
The clouds on their journey above,
The cold wet winds ever blowing,
And the shadowy hazel grove
Where mouse-grey waters are flowing,
Threaten the head that I love.

W.B. YEATS (1865-1939)

Being in Love

with someone who is not in love with
you, you understand my predicament.
Being in love with you, who are not
in love with me, you understand my dilemma.
Being in love with your being in love
with me, which you are not, you understand

the difficulty. Being in love with your
being, you can well imagine how hard it is.
Being in love with your being you,
no matter you are not your being being in
love with me, you can appreciate and pity
being in love with you. Being in love

with someone who is not in love, you know
all about being in love when being in love
is being in love with someone who is not
in love being with you, which is
being in love, which you know only too well,
Love, being in love with being in love.

MARVIN BELL (*b.* 1937)

'When my love swears that she is made of truth'

When my love swears that she is made of truth,
I do believe her though I know she lies,
That she might think me some untutored youth,
Unlearnèd in the world's false subtleties.
Thus vainly thinking that she thinks me young,
Although she knows my days are past the best,
Simply I credit her false-speaking tongue;
On both sides thus is simple truth suppressed.
But wherefore says she not she is unjust?
And wherefore say not I that I am old?
O, love's best habit is in seeming trust,
And age in love loves not to have years told.
    Therefore I lie with her, and she with me,
    And in our faults by lies we flattered be.

WILLIAM SHAKESPEARE (1564-1616)

The Sorrow of Love

I saw my love in his anger
And he didn't pretend to admire.
Yet I am the vein of his heart
And the beauty of his desire.

Oh, fire in the night is my love
When anger his spirit enthralls,
Yet he is kinder to me
Than the lambs who come when I call.

He holds me with both his hands
And swears that he loves me true.
He says I am golder than gold
At the bottom of Sliav Dhu.

But he passed me coldly today
And I wish that the birds wouldn't sing,
And I wish that I was far away
At the rim of the world's ring.

FRANCIS LEDWIDGE (1891-1917)

The Ribbon

I thought she'd taken all her things
But I was wrong. Wherever I go
I catch glimpses of my damnation.

Is that too strong a word? You wouldn't think so
If you could see this lovely ribbon
Wound around my hand.

Don't tell me, I know,
I'm mumbling to myself again. I'm like King Kong
Picking among the ruins of New York
For a clue to his misfortune.

I keep wondering what they were like,
These odds and ends,
Collecting dust, though freed at last from blame.
Did they look the same
When she held them in her hand?

It seems ridiculous
How everything here acknowledges her touch,
Including me, including this tangled ribbon.

Perhaps you were right after all
And I make too much of it. I'll just sit here now
And try to undo these knots –
I'll be with you in a minute, if you can wait.

HUGO WILLIAMS (*b.* 1942)

'With how sad steps, O Moon'

With how sad steps, O Moon, thou climbst the skies!
How silently, and with how wan a face!
What, may it be that even in heavenly place
That busy archer his sharp arrows tries?
Sure, if that long-with-love-acquainted eyes
Can judge of love, thou feel'st a lover's case:
I read it in thy looks: thy languisht grace,
To me that feel the like, thy state descries.
Then even of fellowship, O Moon, tell me,
Is constant love deem'd there but want of wit?
Are beauties there as proud as here they be?
Do they above love to be lov'd, and yet
Those lovers scorn whom that love doth possess?
Do they call virtue there ungratefulness?

SIR PHILIP SIDNEY (1554-86)

The Crack

cut right through the house:
a thick wiggly line
you could poke a finger into,
a deep gash seeping
fine black dust.

It didn't appear overnight.
For a long time
it was such a fine line
we went up and down stairs
oblivious of the stresses

that were splitting
our walls and ceilings apart.
And even when it thickened
and darkened, we went on
not seeing, or seeing

but believing the crack
would heal itself,
if dry earth was to blame,
a winter of rain
would seal its edges.

You didn't tell me
that you heard at night
its faint stirrings
like something alive.
And I didn't tell you –

until the crack
had opened so wide
that if we'd moved in our sleep
to reach for each other
we'd have fallen through.

VICKI FEAVER (*b*. 1943)

Schooner

A tossed night between us
high seas
and then in the morning
sails slack
rope flapping the rigging
your schooner came in

on the deck, buttressed
with mango boxes, chicken-
coops, rice: I saw you:
older than I would wish you
more tattered than my pride
could stand

you saw me
moving reluctant to the quay-
side, stiff as you knew me
too full of pride.
but you had travelled
braved the big wave
and the bilge-swishing stomach,
climbed the tall seas
to come to me

ship was too early
or was I too late?

walking still slowly
(too late or too early?)
saw you suddenly turn

ropes quickly cast off from the capstan
frilled sails were unfurled
water already between your hull and the harbour

too late too late
or too early?

running now
one last rope stretched
to the dockside
tripping over a chain –
chink in my armour –

but the white bows were turning
stern coming round squat in the water

and I
older now
more torn and tattered than my pride
could stand
stretch out my love to you across the water
but cannot reach your hand

KAMAU BRATHWAITE (*b.* 1930)

At Castle Boterel

As I drive to the junction of lane and highway,
    And the drizzle bedrenches the waggonette,
I look behind at the fading byway,
    And see on its slope, now glistening wet,
        Distinctly yet

Myself and a girlish form benighted
    In dry March weather. We climb the road
Beside a chaise. We had just alighted
    To ease the sturdy pony's load
        When he sighed and slowed.

What we did as we climbed, and what we talked of
    Matters not much, nor to what it led, –
Something that life will not be balked of
    Without rude reason till hope is dead,
        And feeling fled.

It filled but a minute. But was there ever
     A time of such quality, since or before,
In that hill's story? To one mind never,
     Though it has been climbed, foot-swift, foot-sore,
          By thousands more.

Primaeval rocks form the road's steep border,
     And much have they faced there, first and last,
Of the transitory in Earth's long order;
     But what they record in colour and cast
          Is – that we two passed.

And to me, though Time's unflinching rigour,
     In mindless rote, has ruled from sight
The substance now, one phantom figure
     Remains on the slope, as when that night
          Saw us alight.

I look and see it there, shrinking, shrinking,
     I look back at it amid the rain
For the very last time; for my sand is sinking,
     And I shall traverse old love's domain
          Never again

THOMAS HARDY (1840-1928)

O Woman

O woman for whom
I have withdrawn

From naming the brilliant things of the earth
Less they might lose their vividness,

Can we now without myth
Sustain the emptiness?

Silence has invaded the house.
The water does not move.

These are the two guilty quiets of all:
A boat at the door, our sealed lips.

I cannot hear the wild duck.
There is only one swan.

The silence of the waters
Goes on and on.

DERMOT HEALY (*b*. 1947)

'Never more will the wind'

Never more will the wind
cherish you again,
never more will the rain.

Never more
shall we find you bright
in the snow and wind.

The snow is melted,
the snow is gone,
and you are flown:

Like a bird out of our hand,
like a light out of our heart,
you are gone.

H.D. (1886-1961)

Odi et amo
(LXXXV)

I hate and I love. Why? You may ask but
It beats me. I feel it done to me, and ache.

CATULLUS (*c*.84-*c*.54 BC)
version from the Latin by Ezra Pound

The Parting: II

White morning flows into the mirror.
Her eye, still old with sleep,
meets itself like a sister.

How they slept last night,
the dream that caged them back to back,
was nothing new.

Last words, tears, most often
come wrapped as the everyday
familiar failure.

Now, pulling the comb slowly
through her loosened hair
she tries to find the parting;

it must come out after all:
hidden in all that tangle
there is a way.

ADRIENNE RICH (*b*. 1929)

When Love Flies in

When Love flies in,
Make – make no sign;
Owl-soft his wings,
Sand-blind his eyne;
Sigh, if thou must,
But seal him thine.

Nor make no sign
If love flit out;
He'll tire of thee
Without a doubt.
Stifle thy pangs;
Thy heart resign;
And live without!

WALTER DE LA MARE (1873-1956)

from Astrophil and Stella

Loving in truth, and fain in verse my love to show,
That she (dear she) might take some pleasure of my pain;
Pleasure might cause her read, reading might make her know;
Knowledge might pity win, and pity grace obtain;
    I sought fit words to paint the blackest face of woe,
Studying inventions fine, her wits to entertain;
Oft turning others' leaves, to see if thence would flow
Some fresh and fruitful showers upon my sunburnt brain.
    But words came halting forth, wanting invention's stay;
Invention, nature's child, fled step-dame study's blows;
And others' feet still seemed but strangers in my way.
Thus, great with child to speak, and helpless in my throes,
    Biting my truant pen, beating myself for spite,
    'Fool,' said my muse to me; 'look in thy heart and write.'

SIR PHILIP SIDNEY (1554-86)

'Thrice toss these oaken ashes in the air'

Thrice toss these oaken ashes in the air,
Thrice sit thou mute in this enchanted chair;
Then thrice three times tie up this true love's knot.
And murmur soft: 'She will, or she will not.'

Go burn these poisonous weeds in yon blue fire,
These screech-owl's feathers and this prickling briar,
This cypress gathered at a dead man's grave,
That all thy fears and cares an end may have.

Then come, you fairies, dance with me a round;
Melt her hard heart with your melodious sound.
In vain are all the charms I can devise;
She hath an art to break them with her eyes.

THOMAS CAMPION (1567-1634)

To Lallie (Outside the British Museum)

Up those Museum steps you came,
And straightway all my blood was flame,
                    O Lallie, Lallie!

The world (I had been feeling low)
In one short moment's space did grow
                    A happy valley.

There was a friend, my friend, with you;
A meagre dame, in peacock blue
                    Apparelled quaintly:

This poet-heart went pit-a-pat;
I bowed and smiled and raised my hat;
                    You nodded – faintly.

My heart was full as full could be;
You had not got a word for me.
                    Not one short greeting;

That nonchalant small nod you gave
(The tyrant's motion to the slave)
                    Sole mark'd our meeting.

Is it so long? Do you forget
That first and last time that we met?
                    The time was summer;

The trees were green, the sky was blue;
Our host presented me to you –
                    A tardy comer,

You look'd demure, but when you spoke
You made a little, funny joke,
                    Yet half pathetic,

Your gown was grey, I recollect,
I think you patronised the sect
                    They call 'aesthetic'.

I brought you strawberries and cream,
I plied you long about a stream
                    With duckweed laden;

We solemnly discussed the – heat
I found you shy and very sweet,
                    A rosebud maiden.

Ah me, today! You passed inside
To where the marble gods abide;
                    Hermes, Apollo,

Sweet Aphrodite, Pan; and where,
For aye reclined, a headless fair
                    Beats all fairs hollow.

And I, I went upon my way,
Well – rather sadder, let us say;
                    The world looked flatter.

I had been sad enough before,
A little less, a little more,
                    What *does* it matter?

AMY LEVY (1861-89)

Blues

i woke up this mornin
sunshine int showin through my door
i woke up this mornin
sunshine int showin through my door
cause the blues is got me
and i int got strength to go no more

i woke up this mornin
clothes still scattered cross the floor
i woke up this mornin
clothes still scattered cross the floor
las night the ride was lovely
but she int comin back for more

sea island sunshine
where are you hidin now
sea island sunshine
where are you hidin now
could a sware i left you in the cupboard
but is only empties mockin at me in there now

empty bottles knockin
laugh like a woman satisfied
empty bottles knockin
laugh like a woman satisfied
she full an left me empty
laughin when i should a cried

this place is empty bottles
this place is a woman satisfied
this place is empty bottles
this place is a woman satisfied
she drink muh sugar water
till muh sunshine died

i woke up this mornin
sunshine int showin underneath my door
i woke up this mornin
sunshine int showin underneath my door
she gone an left me empty
and i should a died...

KAMAU BRATHWAITE (*b.* 1930)

Down by the Salley Gardens

Down by the salley gardens my love and I did meet;
She passed the salley gardens with little snow-white feet.
She bid me take love easy, as the leaves grow on the tree;
But I, being young and foolish, with her would not agree.

In a field by the river my love and I did stand,
And on my leaning shoulder she laid her snow-white hand.
She bid me take life easy, as the grass grows on the weirs;
But I was young and foolish, and now am full of tears.

W.B. YEATS (1865-1939)

I Know What I'm Missing

It's a birdcall from the treeline.
I hear it every day.
It's the loveliest of the songbirds
And I'm glad it comes this way
And I stop to listen
And forget what I've to do
And I know what I'm missing –
My friend
My friend.

It's a fluttering in the palmfronds
With a flash of black and gold.
It's the whistling of the oriole
And its beauty turns me cold
And I stop to listen
And forget what I've to do
And I know what I'm missing –
My friend
My friend.

Do you wonder if I'll remember?
Do you wonder where I'll be?
I'll be home again next winter
And I hope you'll write to me.
When the branches glisten
And the frost is on the avenue
I'll know what I'm missing –
My friend
My friend
I'm missing you.

JAMES FENTON (*b.* 1949)

That Day

This is the desk I sit at
and this is the desk where I love you too much
and this is the typewriter that sits before me
where yesterday only your body sat before me
with its shoulders gathered in like a Greek chorus,
with its tongue like a king making up rules as he goes,
with its tongue quite openly like a cat lapping milk,
with its tongue – both of us coiled in its slippery life.
That was yesterday, that day.

That was the day of your tongue,
your tongue that came from your lips,
two openers, half animals, half birds
caught in the doorway of your heart.
That was the day I followed the king's rules,
passing by your red veins and your blue veins,
my hands down the backbone, down quick like a firepole,
hands between legs where you display your inner knowledge,
where diamond mines are buried and come forth to bury,
come forth more sudden than some reconstructed city.
It is complete within seconds, that monument.
The blood runs underground yet brings forth a tower.
A multitude should gather for such an edifice.
For a miracle one stands in line and throws confetti.
Surely The Press is here looking for headlines.
Surely someone should carry a banner on the sidewalk.
If a bridge is constructed doesn't the mayor cut a ribbon?
If a phenomenon arrives shouldn't the Magi come bearing gifts?
Yesterday was the day I bore gifts for your gift
and came from the valley to meet you on the pavement.
That was yesterday, that day.

That was the day of your face,
your face after love, close to the pillow, a lullaby.
Half asleep beside me letting the old fashioned rocker stop,
our breath became one, became a child-breath together,
while my fingers drew little o's on your shut eyes,
while my fingers drew little smiles on your mouth,
while I drew I LOVE YOU on your chest and its drummer

and whispered, 'Wake up!' and you mumbled in your sleep,
'Sh. We're driving to Cape Cod. We're heading for the Bourne
Bridge. We're circling around the Bourne Circle.' Bourne!
Then I knew you in your dream and prayed of our time
that I would be pierced and you would take root in me
and that I might bring forth your born, might bear
the you or the ghost of you in my little household.
Yesterday I did not want to be borrowed
but this is the typewriter that sits before me
and love is where yesterday is at.

ANNE SEXTON (1928-74)

The Voice

Woman much missed, how you call to me, call to me,
Saying that now you are not as you were
When you had changed from the one who was all to me,
But as at first, when our day was fair.

Can it be you that I hear? Let me view you, then,
Standing as when I drew near to the town
Where you would wait for me: yes, as I knew you then,
Even to the original air-blue gown!

Or is it only the breeze, in its listlessness
Travelling across the wet mead to me here,
You being ever dissolved to wan wistlessness,
Heard no more again far or near?

    Thus I; faltering forward,
    Leaves around me falling,
Wind oozing thin through the thorn from norward,
    And the woman calling.

THOMAS HARDY (1840-1928)

'She who is always in my thoughts'

She who is always in my thoughts prefers
Another man, and does not think of me.
Yet he seeks for another's love, not hers;
And some poor girl is grieving for my sake.
Why then, the devil take
Both her and him; and love; and her; and me.

BHARTRHARI (*7th century*)
translated from the Sanskrit by John Brough

Impossibilities to his Friend

My faithful friend, if you can see
The Fruit to grow up, or the Tree:
If you can see the colour come
Into the blushing Peare, or Plum:
If you can see the water grow
To cakes of Ice, or flakes of Snow:
If you can see, that drop of raine
Lost in the wild sea, once againe:
If you can see, how Dreams do creep
Into the Brain by easie sleep:
Then there is hope that you may see
Her love me once, who now hates me.

ROBERT HERRICK (1591-1674)

'He would not stay for me'

He would not stay for me; and who can wonder?
  He would not stay for me to stand and gaze.
I shook his hand and tore my heart in sunder
  And went with half my life about my ways.

A.E. HOUSMAN (1859-1936)

Another Unfortunate Choice

I think I am in love with A.E. Housman,
Which puts me in a worse-than-usual fix.
No woman ever stood a chance with Housman
And he's been dead since 1936.

WENDY COPE (*b.* 1945)

I Am No Good at Love

I am no good at love
My heart should be wise and free
I kill the unfortunate golden goose
Whoever it may be
With over-articulate tenderness
And too much intensity.

I am no good at love
I batter it out of shape
Suspicion tears at my sleepless mind
And, gibbering like an ape,
I lie alone in the endless dark
Knowing there's no escape.

I am no good at love
When my easy heart I yield
Wild words come tumbling from my mouth
Which should have stayed concealed;
And my jealousy turns a bed of bliss
Into a battlefield.

I am no good at love
I betray it with little sins
For I feel the misery of the end
In the moment that it begins
And the bitterness of the last goodbye
Is the bitterness that wins.

NOEL COWARD (1899-1973)

Love without Hope

Love without hope, as when the young bird-catcher
Swept off his tall hat to the Squire's own daughter,
So let the imprisoned larks escape and fly
Singing about her head, as she rode by.

ROBERT GRAVES (1895-1985)

Warming Her Pearls

Next to my own skin, her pearls. My mistress
bids me wear them, warm them, until evening
when I'll brush her hair. At six, I place them
round her cool, white throat. All day I think of her,

resting in the Yellow Room, contemplating silk
or taffeta, which gown tonight? She fans herself
whilst I work willingly, my slow heat entering
each pearl. Slack on my neck, her rope.

She's beautiful. I dream about her
in my attic bed; picture her dancing
with tall men, puzzled by my faint, persistent scent
beneath her French perfume, her milky stones.

I dust her shoulders with a rabbit's foot,
watch the soft blush seep through her skin
like an indolent sigh. In her looking-glass
my red lips part as though I want to speak.

Full moon. Her carriage brings her home. I see
her every movement in my head...Undressing,
taking off her jewels, her slim hand reaching
for the case, slipping naked into bed, the way

she always does...And I lie here awake,
knowing the pearls are cooling even now
in the room where my mistress sleeps. All night
I feel their absence and I burn.

CAROL ANN DUFFY (*b.* 1955)

The Farmer's Bride

Three Summers since I chose a maid,
Too young maybe – but more's to do
At harvest-time than bide and woo.
        When us was wed she turned afraid
Of love and me and all things human;
Like the shut of a winter's day.
Her smile went out, and 'twasn't a woman –
    More like a little frightened fay.
        One night, in the Fall, she runned away.

233

'Out 'mong the sheep, her be,' they said,
  'Should properly have been abed;
  But sure enough she wasn't there
  Lying awake with her wide brown stare.
So over seven-acre field and up-along across the down
  We chased her, flying like a hare
  Before our lanterns. To Church-Town
    All in a shiver and a scare
  We caught her, fetched her home at last
    And turned the key upon her, fast.

She does the work about the house
  As well as most, but like a mouse:
    Happy enough to cheat and play
    With birds and rabbits and such as they,
    So long as men-folk keep away.
  'Not near, not near!' her eyes beseech
  When one of us comes within reach.
    The women say that beasts in stall
    Look round like children at her call.
    I've hardly heard her speak at all.

Shy as a leveret, swift as he,
Straight and slight as a young larch tree,
Sweet as the first wild violets, she,
To her wild self. But what to me?

The short days shorten and the oaks are brown,
  The blue smoke rises to the low grey sky,
One leaf in the still air falls slowly down,
  A magpie's spotted feathers lie
On the black earth spread white with rime,
The berries redden up to Christmas-time.
  What's Christmas-time without there be
  Some other in the house than we!

She sleeps up in the attic there
  Alone, poor maid. 'Tis but a stair
Betwixt us. Oh! my God! the down
The soft young down of her, the brown,
The brown of her – her eyes, her hair, her hair!

CHARLOTTE MEW (1869-1928)

A Plain Girl

A plain girl moving simply enough
Until love turned her down flat,
Leaving her with her parents' lives to live
And trunk full of embroidered stuff.

She acknowledged her plainness thereafter,
Underlined it rigorously
With all the farm work she could find.
Forgot the knack of easy laughter.

Her sisters watched how her coarseness grew,
Saw time-killing work broaden her hands
And gait, watched her gather a man's strength
To herself in the only way that she knew.

Guardedly her brothers watched her come and go,
Kept an eye on her many distances
As though she were the unpredictable horse
They enclosed in the furthest meadow.

Her meagre words the family understood
And they never forgot to turn away
When, with a quiet ferocity,
She chopped unnecessary piles of wood.

FREDA DOWNIE (1929-93)

Vinegar

sometimes
i feel like a priest
in a fish & chip queue
quietly thinking
as the vinegar runs through
how nice it would be
to buy supper for two

ROGER McGOUGH (*b*. 1937)

'Whoso list to hunt'

Whoso list to hunt, I know where is an hind,
But as for me, helas, I may no more.
The vain travail hath wearied me so sore,
I am of them that farthest come behind.
Yet may I by no means my wearied mind
Draw from the Deer, but as she fleeth afore
Fainting I follow. I leave off therefore,
Since in a net I seek to hold the wind.
Who list her hunt (I put him out of doubt)
As well as I may spend his time in vain.
And graven with diamonds in letters plain
There is written her fair neck round about:
'Noli me tangere, for Caesar's I am,
And wild for to hold, though I seem tame.'

SIR THOMAS WYATT (1503-42)

Delay

The radiance of that star that leans on me
Was shining years ago. The light that now
Glitters up there my eye may never see,
And so the time lag teases me with how

Love that loves now may not reach me until
Its first desire is spent. The star's impulse
Must wait for eyes to claim it beautiful
And love arrived may find us somewhere else.

ELIZABETH JENNINGS (1926-2001)

Snow Melting

Snow melting when I left you, and I took
This fragile bone we'd found in melting snow
Before I left, exposed beside a brook
Where raccoons washed their hands. And this, I know,

Is that raccoon we'd watched for every day.
Though at the time her wild human hand
Had gestured inexplicably, I say
Her meaning now is more than I can stand.

We've reasons, we have reasons, so we say,
For giving love, and for withholding it.
I who would love must marvel at the way
I know aloneness when I'm holding it,

Know near and far as words for live and die,
Know distance, as I'm trying to draw near,
Growing immense, and know, but don't know why,
Things seen up close enlarge, then disappear.

Tonight this small room seems too huge to cross.
And my life is that looming kind of place.
Here, left with this alone, and at a loss
I hold an alien and vacant face

Which shrinks away, and yet is magnified –
More so than I seem able to explain.
Tonight the giant galaxies outside
Are tiny, tiny on my windowpane.

GJERTRUD SCHNACKENBERG (*b.* 1953)

Across

Across these miles I wish you well.
May nothing haunt your heart but sleep.
May you not sense what I don't tell.
May you not dream, or doubt, or weep.

May what my pen this peaceless day
Writes on this page not reach your view
Till its deferred print lets you say
It speaks to someone else than you.

VIKRAM SETH (*b.* 1952)

Lepidopterist

'I've done my best to immortalise what I failed to keep.'
– JOSEPH BRODSKY

And now I am a lepidopterist
with my rows of bitter pins
securing here, now there
the flown species wings.

If we soak the memories
in our bile
they will keep and crystallise
come clear
in the heat of this now poisoned air.
I thought I had you/where are you?
You gave up on us/I gave up on you
You changed your mind/I'm changing mine
Lord, even in death the wings beat so.
Hold still
let me put this last row in.

LORNA GOODISON (*b.* 1947)

The Train

I've been trying, my darling, to explain
to myself how it is that some freight train
loaded with ballast so a track may rest
easier in its bed should be what's roused

us both from ours, tonight as every night,
despite its being miles off and despite
our custom of putting to the very
back of the mind all that's customary

and then, since it takes forever to pass
with its car after car of coal and gas
and salt and wheat and rails and railway ties,

how it seems determined to give the lie
to the notion, my darling,
that we, not it, might be the constant thing.

PAUL MULDOON (*b.* 1952)

K563

As on most fine summer Sundays
we are breakfasting outdoors with our books.
This morning it is one of the Divertimenti
keeps the neighbours to themselves.
Now I can remember that man's name – Puchberg –
who funded Mozart when his wife was ill
        and the money coming in
wasn't covering the bills.
This is Vienna in 1788 in sunlight.

What are we supposed to do?
I open a conversation about Mozart
and you look up from the Penguin biography.
        The sky is a Prussian blue
and our back-yard garden is lit with music.

We are not yet thirty, and our lives
        are just about to start.
There is someone new, but that
is not why you are leaving. The cat,
who will be staying, stalks a daytime moth;
two stray poppies add a splash of colour.

It is very civilised. We are parting like friends.
On the breeze the churchbell tolls eleven.
Coming so far he won't arrive till three,
but your cases are already packed in case.
I've not slept properly for days
and now I need to be awake I find I'm dozing.
        When the record finishes
it is the hairfine crack in a teacup, ticking,
or a clock, perhaps, loud and very exact.

PETER SANSOM (*b.* 1958)

240

Don't Think Twice, It's All Right

It ain't no use to sit and wonder why, babe
It don't matter, anyhow
An' it ain't no use to sit and wonder why, babe
If you don't know by now
When your rooster crows at the break of dawn
Look out your window and I'll be gone
You're the reason I'm trav'lin' on
Don't think twice, it's all right

It ain't no use in turnin' on your light, babe
That light I never knowed
An' it ain't no use in turnin' on your light, babe
I'm on the dark side of the road
Still I wish there was somethin' you would do or say
To try and make me change my mind and stay
We never did too much talkin' anyway
So don't think twice, it's all right

It ain't no use in callin' out my name, gal
Like you never did before
It ain't no use in callin' out my name, gal
I can't hear you any more
I'm a-thinkin' and a-wond'rin' all the way down the road
I once loved a woman, a child I'm told
I give her my heart but she wanted my soul
But don't think twice, it's all right

I'm walkin' down that long, lonesome road, babe
Where I'm bound, I can't tell
But goodbye's too good a word, gal
So I'll just say fare thee well
I ain't sayin' you treated me unkind
You could have done better but I don't mind
You just kinda wasted my precious time
But don't think twice, it's all right

BOB DYLAN (*b*. 1941)

241

No Second Troy

Why should I blame her that she filled my days
With misery, or that she would of late
Have taught to ignorant men most violent ways,
Or hurled the little streets upon the great,
Had they but courage equal to desire?
What could have made her peaceful with a mind
That nobleness made simple as a fire,
With beauty like a tightened bow, a kind
That is not natural in an age like this,
Being high and solitary and most stern?
Why, what could she have done, being what she is?
Was there another Troy for her to burn?

W.B. YEATS (1865-1939)

11

'The end of love'

(SOPHIE HANNAH)

'So we'll go no more a-roving'

So we'll go no more a-roving
    So late into the night,
Though the heart be still as loving,
    And the moon be still as bright.

For the sword outwears its sheath,
    And the soul wears out the breast,
And the heart must pause to breathe,
    And Love itself have rest.

Though the night was made for loving,
    And the day returns too soon,
Yet we'll go no more a-roving
    By the light of the moon.

LORD BYRON (1788-1824)

I Threw It All Away

I once held her in my arms,
She said she would always stay.
But I was cruel,
I treated her like a fool,
I threw it all away.

Once I had mountains in the palm of my hand,
And rivers that ran through ev'ry day.
I must have been mad,
I never knew what I had,
Until I threw it all away.

Love is all there is, it makes the world go 'round,
Love and only love, it can't be denied.
No matter what you think about it
You just won't be able to do without it.
Take a tip from one who's tried.

So if you find someone that gives you all of her love,
Take it to your heart, don't let it stray,
For one thing that's certain,
You will surely be a-hurtin',
If you throw it all away.

BOB DYLAN (*b.* 1941)

Separation

Stop! – not to me, at this bitter departing,
    Speak of the sure consolations of time!
Fresh be the wound, still-renew'd be its smarting,
    So but thy image endure in its prime.

But, if the stedfast commandment of Nature
    Wills that remembrance should always decay –
If the loved form and the deep-cherish'd feature
    Must, when unseen, from the soul fade away –

Me let no half-effaced memories cumber!
    Fled, fled at once, be all vestige of thee!
Deep be the darkness and still be the slumber –
    Dead be the past and its phantoms to me!

Then, when we meet, and thy look strays toward me,
    Scanning my face and the changes wrought there:
Who, let me say, *is this stranger regards me,*
    With the grey eyes, and the lovely brown hair?

MATTHEW ARNOLD (1822-88)

Farewell

What should I say,
   Since faith is dead,
And truth away
   From you is fled:
   Should I be led
      With doubleness?
      Nay, nay, mistress!

I promised you,
   And you promised me,
To be as true,
   As I would be.
   But since I see
      Your double heart,
      Farewell my part!

Thought for to take
   It is not my mind,
But to forsake
   One so unkind,
   And as I find
      So will I trust,
      Farewell, unjust!

Can ye say nay,
   But that you said
That I alway
   Should be obeyed?
   And thus betrayed,
      Or that I wist,
      Farewell, unkissed!

SIR THOMAS WYATT (1503-42)

La Belle Dame sans Merci

O what can ail thee, knight-at-arms,
   Alone and palely loitering?
The sedge has wither'd from the lake,
   And no birds sing.

O what can ail thee, knight-at-arms,
   So haggard and so woe-begone?
The squirrel's granary is full,
   And the harvest's done.

I see a lilly on thy brow,
   With anguish moist and fever dew;
And on thy cheeks a fading rose
   Fast withereth too.

I met a lady in the meads,
   Full beautiful – a faery's child,
Her hair was long, her foot was light,
   And her eyes were wild.

I made a garland for her head,
   And bracelets too, and fragrant zone;
She look'd at me as she did love,
   And made sweet moan.

I set her on my pacing steed,
   And nothing else saw all day long,
For sidelong would she bend, and sing
   A faery's song.

She found me roots of relish sweet,
   And honey wild, and manna dew,
And sure in language strange she said –
   'I love thee true'.

She took me to her elfin grot,
   And there she wept, and sigh'd full sore,
And there I shut her wild wild eyes
   With kisses four.

And there she lulled me asleep,
  And there I dream'd – Ah! woe betide!
The latest dream I ever dream'd
  On the cold hill side.

I saw pale kings and princes too,
  Pale warriors, deathpale were they all;
They cried – 'La Belle Dame sans Merci
  Hath thee in thrall!'

I saw their starved lips in the gloam,
  With horrid warning gaped wide,
And I awoke and found me here,
  On the cold hill's side.

And this is why I sojourn here,
  Alone and palely loitering,
Though the sedge has wither'd from the lake,
  And no birds sing.

JOHN KEATS (1795-1821)

Of No Use

No. You've never needed my gestures
tied up like ribbons round some handle,
or my eyes embroidered on the fixtures,
or my whole playful universe.

You never needed that heavenly bliss
of words – or the absolute yearning
whose pale chisel carved
the stone of moments into the shape of a kiss.

I was no use to you – it was like seasons that pass
in reverse, twos, threes or fours,
like rain trying to fill a glass,
or ruining books when it pours.

NINA CASSIAN (b. 1924)
translated from the Romanian by Brenda Walker & Andrea Deletant

'I would like my love to die'

I would like my love to die
and the rain to be raining on the graveyard
and on me walking the streets
mourning her who thought she loved me

SAMUEL BECKETT (1906-89)

'They flee from me that sometime did me seek'

They flee from me that sometime did me seek
   With naked foot stalking in my chamber.
I have seen them gentle, tame and meek
    That now are wild and do not remember
    That sometime they put themselves in danger
To take bread at my hand; and now they range
Busily seeking with a continual change.

Thanked be fortune, it hath been otherwise
   Twenty times better; but once in special,
In thin array after a pleasant guise,
    When her loose gown from her shoulders did fall,
    And she me caught in her arms long and small;
Therewith all sweetly did me kiss,
And softly said, *'Dear heart, how like you this?'*

It was no dream: I lay broad waking.
   But all is turned thorough my gentleness
Into a strange fashion of forsaking,
    And I have leave to go of her goodness,
    And she also to use newfangleness.
But since that I so kindly am served,
I would fain know what she hath deserved.

SIR THOMAS WYATT (1503-42)

Merciles Beaute

(a triple roundel)

I [CAPTIVITY]

Your yen two wol slee me sodenly;
I may the beautee of hem not sustene,
So woundeth hit thourghout my herte kene.

And but your word wol helen hastily
My hertes wounde, while that hit is grene,
   Your yen two wol slee me sodenly;
    I may the beautee of hem not sustene.

Upon my trouthe I sey you feithfully
That ye ben of my lyf and deeth the quene;
For with my deeth the trouthe shal be sene.
   Your yen two wol slee me sodenly;
    I may the beautee of hem not sustene,
    So woundeth hit thourghout my herte kene.

II [REJECTION]

So hath your beautee fro your herte chaced
Pitee, that me ne availeth not to pleyne;
For Daunger halt your mercy in his cheyne.

Giltles my deeth thus han ye me purchaced;
I sey you sooth, me nedeth not to feyne;
   So hath your beautee fro your herte chaced
    Pitee, that me ne availeth not to pleyne.

Allas! that Nature hath in you compassed
So greet beautee, that no man may atteyne
To mercy, though he sterve for the peyne.
   So hath your beautee fro your herte chaced
    Pitee, that me ne availeth not to pleyne;
    For Daunger halt your mercy in his cheyne.

III [ESCAPE]

Sin I fro Love escaped am so fat,
I never thenk to ben in his prison lene;
Sin I am free, I counte him not a bene.

He may answere, and seye this or that;
I do no fors, I speke right as I mene.
   Sin I fro Love escaped am so fat,
   I never thenk to ben in his prison lene.

Love hath my name ystrike out of his sclat,
And he is strike out of my bokes clene
For ever-mo; ther is non other mene.
   Sin I fro Love escaped am so fat,
   I never thenk to ben in his prison lene;
   Sin I am free, I counte him not a bene.

GEOFFREY CHAUCER [?] (c.1343-1400)

The End of Love

The end of love should be a big event.
It should involve the hiring of a hall.
Why the hell not? It happens to us all.
Why should it pass without acknowledgement?

Suits should be dry-cleaned, invitations sent.
Whatever form it takes – a tiff, a brawl –
The end of love should be a big event.
It should involve the hiring of a hall.

Better than the unquestioning descent
Into the trap of silence, than the crawl
From visible to hidden, door to wall.

Get the announcements made, the money spent.
The end of love should be a big event.
It should involve the hiring of a hall.

SOPHIE HANNAH (b. 1971)

'Since there's no help'

Since there's no help, come let us kiss and part, –
Nay I have done, you get no more of me;
And I am glad, yea glad with all my heart,
That thus so cleanly I myself can free;
Shake hands forever, cancel all our vows,
And when we meet at any time again,
Be it not seen in either of our brows
That we one jot of former love retain.
Now at the last gasp of Love's latest breath,
When, his pulse failing, Passion speechless lies,
When Faith is kneeling by his bed of death,
And Innocence is closing up his eyes, –
Now if though would'st, when all have given him over,
From death to life thou might'st him yet recover!

MICHAEL DRAYTON (1563-1631)

I have cut from my heart

I have cut from my heart
her green-sickness;
it is better to be a tall and lonely man
than stand and cry for the moon.

The moon is older than the sun.
Why should a man set his soul
in the house of a girl?
To be alive is to be alone.

It is better to look and turn away.
She is beautiful where she walks;
she is beautiful where she stands;
as any flowering tree.

JAMES K. BAXTER (1926-72)

Love: The Dance

They're not quite overdressed, just a bit attentively, flashily for
    seventy-five or eighty.
Both wear frosted, frozen, expensive but still delicately balanced and
    just-adhering wigs,
and both have heavy makeup: his could pass for a Miami winter tan,
    but hers goes off the edge –
ice-pink lipstick, badly drawn, thick mascara arching like a ballerina's
    toward the brow.
All things considered, she's not built that badly; he has his gut
    sucked nearly neatly in;
their dancing is flamboyant, well rehearsed, old-time ballroom swirls,
    deft romantic dips and bows.
If only they wouldn't contrive to catch our eyes so often, to acknow-
    ledge with ingratiating grins:
the waltz of life, the waltz of death, and still the heart-work left
    undone, the heavy heart, left undone.

C.K. WILLIAMS (b. 1936)

from By Grand Central Station
I Sat Down and Wept

Under the redwood tree my grave was laid, and I beguiled my true
love to lie down. The stream of our kiss put a waterway around
the world, where love like a refugee sailed in the last ship. My
hair made a shroud, and kept the coyotes at bay while we wrote
our cyphers with anatomy. The winds boomed triumph, our spines
seemed overburdened, and our bones groaned like old trees, but a
smile like a cobweb was fastened across the mouth of the cave of
fate.

ELIZABETH SMART (1913–86)

Don't Pinch Me, Hurts

'Don't pinch me, hurts,'...
you said, a slight frown on your brow.

'Hurts', a perfect sphere half spat out,
on the tip of your tongue it rolls – pirouettes.

One glance and you have spoken.
Secrets float
swirling into the glint of your eyes.

Dreams
shower spreading
a mesh made of chiffon.

'Where are you?'
'Let us die,' you said.

XU ZHI MO (1897-1931)
translated from the Chinese by Carolyn Choa

Sonnet of the Sweet Complaint

I am afraid to lose the miracle
of your eyes – like a statue's – and the voice
which strokes my cheek, a thing nocturnal,
your breathing's solitary rose.

I have the pain of being on this shore,
trunk without branches. What I most regret
is having neither pulp, nor clay, nor flower
to feed the earthworm of my hurt.

If you are my hidden treasure,
if you're my cross, my tear-soaked grief,
if I am your lordship's dog,

don't let me lose what I have gained
and decorate the waters of your river
with my abandoned autumn's leaf.

FEDERICO GARCÍA LORCA (1899-1936)
translated from the Spanish by Merryn Williams

Winter

The tree still bends over the lake,
And I try to recall our love,
Our love which had a thousand leaves.

SHEILA WINGFIELD (1906 92)

Retrospect

Wanting some yourself
you offer me cherries.
Girlish again
you hang a pair over your ear
pale where they touched
as your breasts were.

Wanting memories
you hold out a wishbone stalk
to split between us.

But I want my time back.
Give me back
the pressure of my hands.

PETER DALE (*b.* 1938)

Out of Danger

Heart be kind and sign the release
As the trees their loss approve.
Learn as leaves must learn to fall
Out of danger, out of love.

What belongs to frost and thaw
Sullen winter will not harm.
What belongs to wind and rain
Is out of danger from the storm.

Jealous passion, cruel need
Betray the heart they feed upon.
But what belongs to earth and death
Is out of danger from the sun.

I was cruel, I was wrong –
Hard to say and hard to know.
You do not belong to me.
You are out of danger now –

Out of danger from the wind,
Out of danger from the wave,
Out of danger from the heart
Falling, falling out of love.

JAMES FENTON (*b.* 1949)

A Breath of Air

I walked, when love was gone,
Out of the human town,
For an easy breath of air.
Beyond a break in the trees,
Beyond the hangdog lives
Of old men, beyond girls:
The tall stars held their peace.
Looking in vain for lies
I turned, like earth, to go.
An owl's wings hovered, bare
On the moon's hills of snow.

And things were as they were.

JAMES WRIGHT (1927-80)

12

'What will survive of us is love'

(PHILIP LARKIN)

She's Like the Swallow

She's like the swallow that flies so high,
She's like the river that never runs dry,
She's like the sunshine on the lee shore,
I love my love and love is no more.

'Twas out in the garden this fair maid did go,
A-picking the beautiful prim-e-rose;
The more she plucked the more she pulled
Until she got her a-per-on full.

It's out of the roses she made a bed,
A stony pillow for her head.
She laid her down, no word did say,
Until this fair maid's heart did break.

She's like the swallow that flies so high,
She's like the river that never runs dry,
She's like the sunshine on the lee shore,
I love my love and love is no more.

TRADITIONAL

Frankie and Johnny

Frankie and Johnny were lovers.
O my Gawd how they did love!
They swore to be true to each other,
As true as the stars above.
He was her man but he done her wrong.

Frankie went down to the hock-shop,
Went for a bucket of beer,
Said: 'O Mr Bartender
Has my loving Johnny been here?
He is my man but he's doing me wrong.'

'I don't want to make you no trouble,
I don't want to tell you no lie,
But I saw Johnny an hour ago
With a girl named Nelly Bly,
He is your man but he's doing you wrong.'

Frankie went down to the hotel,
She didn't go there for fun,
'Cause underneath her kimona
She toted a 44 Gun.
He was her man but he done her wrong.

Frankie went down to the hotel.
She rang the front-door bell,
Said: 'Stand back all you chippies
Or I'll blow you all to hell.
I want my man for he's doing me wrong.'

Frankie looked in through the key-hole
And there before her eye
She saw her Johnny on the sofa
A-loving up Nelly Bly.
He was her man; he was doing her wrong.

Frankie threw back her kimona,
Took out a big 44,
Root-a-toot-toot, three times she shot
Right through that hardware door.
He was her man but he was doing her wrong.

Johnny grabbed up his Stetson,
Said: 'O my Gawd Frankie don't shoot!'
But Frankie pulled hard on the trigger
And the gun went root-a-toot-toot.
She shot her man who was doing her wrong.

'Roll me over easy,
Roll me over slow,
Roll me over on my right side
Cause my left side hurts me so.
I was her man but I done her wrong.'

'Bring out your rubber-tired buggy,
Bring out your rubber-tired hack;
I'll take my Johnny to the graveyard
But I won't bring him back.
He was my man but he done me wrong.

'Lock me in that dungeon,
Lock me in that cell,
Lock me where the north-east wind
Blows from the corner of Hell.
I shot my man 'cause he done me wrong.'

It was not murder in the first degree,
It was not murder in the third.
A woman simply shot her man
As a hunter drops a bird.
She shot her man 'cause he done her wrong.

Frankie said to the Sheriff,
'What do you think they'll do?'
The Sheriff said to Frankie,
'It's the electric-chair for you.
You shot your man 'cause he done you wrong.'

Frankie sat in the jail-house,
Had no electric fan,
Told her sweet little sister:
'There ain't no good in a man.
I had a man but he done me wrong.'

Once more I saw Frankie,
She was sitting in the Chair
Waiting for to go and meet her God
With the sweat dripping out of her hair.
He was a man but he done her wrong.

This story has no moral,
This story has no end,
This story only goes to show
That there ain't no good in men.
He was her man but he done her wrong.

ANONYMOUS

Donal Og

It is late last night the dog was speaking of you;
the snipe was speaking of you in her deep marsh.
It is you are the lonely bird through the woods;
and that you may be without a mate until you find me.

You promised me, and you said a lie to me,
that you would be before me where the sheep are flocked;
I gave a whistle and three hundred cries to you,
and I found nothing there but a bleating lamb.

You promised me a thing that was hard for you,
a ship of gold under a silver mast;
twelve towns with a market in all of them,
and a fine white court by the side of the sea.

You promised me a thing that is not possible,
that you would give me gloves of the skin of a fish;
that you would give me shoes of the skin of a bird;
and a suit of the dearest silk in Ireland.

When I go by myself to the Well of Loneliness,
I sit down and I go through my trouble;
when I see the world and do not see my boy,
he that has an amber shade in his hair.

It was on that Sunday I gave my love to you;
the Sunday that is last before Easter Sunday.
And myself on my knees reading the Passion;
and my two eyes giving love to you for ever.

My mother said to me not to be talking with you today,
or tomorrow, or on the Sunday;
it was a bad time she took for telling me that;
it was shutting the door after the house was robbed.

My heart is as black as the blackness of the sloe,
or as the black coal that is on the smith's forge;
or as the sole of a shoe left in white halls;
it was you put that darkness over my life.

You have taken the east from me; you have taken the west from me;
you have taken what is before me and what is behind me;
you have taken the moon, you have taken the sun from me;
and my fear is great that you have taken God from me!

ANONYMOUS
translated from the Irish by Lady Augusta Gregory

Funeral Blues

Stop all the clocks, cut off the telephone,
Prevent the dog from barking with a juicy bone,
Silence the pianos and with muffled drum
Bring out the coffin, let the mourners come.

Let aeroplanes circle moaning overhead
Scribbling on the sky the message He Is Dead,
Put crêpe bows round the white necks of the public doves,
Let the traffic policemen wear black cotton gloves.

He was my North, my South, my East and West,
My working week and my Sunday rest,
My noon, my midnight, my talk, my song;
I thought that love would last for ever: I was wrong.

The stars are not wanted now: put out every one;
Pack up the moon and dismantle the sun;
Pour away the ocean and sweep up the wood.
For nothing now can ever come to any good.

W.H. AUDEN (1907-73)

from **Where you are**

flung to your salt parameters   in all that wide gleam
unbounded edgeless   in that brilliant intersection

where we poured   the shattered grit the salt
and distillation of you   which blew back

into my face stinging   like a kiss
from the other world   a whole year

you've languished blue   in ceaseless wind
naked now in all lights   and chill swaddlings

of cloud never for a moment   cold you are
uninterruptable seamless   as if all this time

you'd been sleeping   in the sparkle and beckon
of it are you   in the pour of it

as if there were a secret   shining room
in the house and you'd   merely gone there

we used to swim   summers remember
naked in those shoals   now I think was I ever

that easy   in this life
fireworks remember   Handel an orchestra

on a barge   in the harbour and fountains
spun to darkness   flung in time to

the music scrawling heaven   like sperm like
chrysanthemums bursting   in an enormous hurry

all fire and chatter   flintspark and dazzle
and utterly gone   save here in the scribble

of winter sunlight   on sheer mercury,
when I was a child   some green Fourth

flares fretting   the blue-black night
a twirling bit of ash   fell in my open eye

and for a while I couldn't see   those skyrockets
is it like that now love   some cinder

blocking my sight   so that I can't see you
who are only for an hour   asleep and dreaming

in this blue   and light-shot room
as if I could lean across   this shifting watery bed

and ask   are you awake

MARK DOTY (*b.* 1953)

Lacuna

sometimes still I turn to the phone
thinking I'll disturb you room to room
only to seize before I'm there
to remember that you've gone

the words I wake will not strike home
but only stray into starless air

absurd I'll not reach you again
and that there's no one now to miss

those that remain remain
in other countries
in their own time, with their own rain

PETER JOLLIFFE (*b.* 1947)

All You Who Sleep Tonight

All you who sleep tonight
Far from the ones you love,
No hand to left or right,
And emptiness above –

Know that you aren't alone.
The whole world shares your tears,
Some for two nights or one,
And some for all their years.

VIKRAM SETH (*b*. 1952)

She Warns Him

I am a lamp, a lamp that is out;
    I am a shallow stream
In it are neither pearls or trout,
    Nor one of the things that you dream.

Why do you smile and deny, my lover?
    I will not be denied
I am a book, a book with a cover
    And nothing at all inside.

Here is the truth, and you must grapple,
    Grapple with what I have said.
I am a dumpling without any apple,
    I am a star that is dead.

FRANCES CORNFORD (1886-1960)

All Soul's Night

My love came back to me
Under the November tree
Shelterless and dim
He put his hand upon my shoulder,
He did not think me strange or older,
Nor I, him.

FRANCES CORNFORD (1886-1960)

Music, When Soft Voices Die

Music, when soft voices die,
Vibrates in the memory –
Odours, when sweet violets sicken,
Live within the sense they quicken.

Rose leaves, when the rose is dead,
Are heaped for the belovèd's bed;
And so thy thoughts, when thou art gone,
Love itself shall slumber on.

PERCY BYSSHE SHELLEY (1792-1822)

One Day I Wrote Her Name Upon the Strand

One day I wrote her name upon the strand,
But came the waves and washèd it away:
Again I wrote it with a second hand,
But came the tide, and made my pains his prey.
Vain man, said she, that dost in vain assay,
A mortal thing so to immortalise,
For I myself shall like to this decay,
And eke my name be wipèd out likewise.
Not so (quoth I), let baser things devise
To die in dust, but you shall live by fame:
My verse your virtues rare shall eternise,
And in the heavens write your glorious name.
   Where whenas death shall all the world subdue,
   Our love shall live, and later life renew.

EDMUND SPENSER (*c*.1552-99)

Love lives beyond the Tomb

   Love lives beyond
The tomb, the earth, which fades like dew –
   I love the fond,
The faithful, and the true.

   Love lies in sleep,
The happiness of healthy dreams,
   Eve's dews may weep,
But love delightful seems.

   'Tis seen in flowers,
And in the even's pearly dew
   On earth's green hours,
And in the heaven's eternal blue.

'Tis heard in spring
When light and sunbeams, warm and kind,
    On angel's wing
Bring love and music to the wind.

    And where is voice
So young, so beautiful, and sweet
    As nature's choice.
Where spring and lovers meet?

    Love lives beyond
The tomb, the earth, the flowers, and dew.
    I love the fond,
The faithful, young, and true.

JOHN CLARE (1793-1864)

A Question

I asked if I got sick and died, would you
With my black funeral go walking too,
If you'd stand close to hear them talk or pray
While I'm let down in that steep bank of clay.

And, No, you said, for if you saw a crew
Of living idiots, pressing round that new
Oak coffin – they alive, I dead beneath
That board – you'd rave and rend them with your teeth.

J.M. SYNGE (1871-1909)

Madrigal

Your love is dead, lady, your love is dead;
Dribbles no sound
From his stopped lips, though swift underground
Spurts his wild hair.

Your love is dead, lady, your love is dead;
Faithless he lies
Deaf to your call, though shades of his eyes
Break through and stare.

R.S. THOMAS (1913-2000)

I Dreamt that you were not Dead

I dreamt last night that Phyllis had come back
in all her earthly beauty lit by day
desired now a ghost to make love once again
for me like Ixion to wed a cloud

Her naked shadow slips into my bed
and says to me 'Dear Damon I am back
I am more beautiful for having been away
in that sad kingdom to which death took me

I come to know again my fairest lover
I come to perish in your arms again'
And when the spirit had abused my flame

she said 'God be with you' I go back to the dead
How you gloried when you had my body
Now you can boast it was my soul you had

CHARLES BAUDELAIRE (1821-67)
translated from the French by Patrick Hope

The Lament for Arthur O'Leary

Eileen speaks:

I

My love forever!
The day I first saw you
At the end of the market-house,
My eye observed you,
My heart approved you,
I fled from my father with you,
Far from my home with you.

II

I never repented it:
You whitened a parlour for me,
Painted rooms for me,
Reddened ovens for me,
Baked fine bread for me,
Basted meat for me,
Slaughtered beasts for me;
I slept in ducks' feathers
Till midday milking-time,
Or more if it pleased me.

III

My friend forever!
My mind remembers
That fine spring day
How well your hat suited you,
Bright gold banded,
Sword silver-hilted –
Right hand steady –
Threatening aspect –
Trembling terror
On treacherous enemy –
You poised for a canter
On your slender bay horse.
The Saxons bowed to you,
Down to the ground to you,
Not for love of you

But for deadly fear of you,
Though you lost your life to them,
Oh my soul's darling.

IV

Oh white-handed rider!
How fine your brooch was
Fastened in cambric,
And your hat with laces.
When you crossed the sea to us,
They would clear the street for you,
And not for love of you
But for deadly hatred.

V

My friend you were forever!
When they will come home to me,
Gentle little Conor
And Farr O'Leary, the baby,
They will question me so quickly,
Where did I leave their father.
I'll answer in my anguish
That I left him in Killnamartyr.
They will call out to their father;
And he won't be there to answer.

VI

My friend and my love!
Of the blood of Lord Antrim,
And of Barry of Allchoill,
How well your sword suited you,
Hat gold-banded,
Boots of fine leather,
Coat of broadcloth,
Spun overseas for you.

VII

My friend you were forever!
I knew nothing of your murder
Till your horse came to the stable
With the reins beneath her trailing,
And your heart's blood on her shoulders

Staining the tooled saddle
Where you used to sit and stand.
My first leap reached the threshold,
My second reached the gateway,
My third leap reached the saddle.

VIII

I struck my hands together
And I made the bay horse gallop
As fast as I was able,
Till I found you dead before me
Beside a little furze-bush.
Without Pope or bishop,
Without priest or cleric
To read the death-psalms for you,
But a spent old woman only
Who spread her cloak to shroud you –
Your heart's blood was still flowing;
I did not stay to wipe it
But filled my hands and drank it.

IX

My love you'll be forever!
Rise up from where you're lying
And we'll be going homewards.
We'll have a bullock slaughtered,
We'll call our friends together,
We'll get the music going.
I'll make a fine bed ready
With sheets of snow-white linen,
And fine embroidered covers
That will bring the sweat out through you
Instead of the cold that's on you!

Arthur O'Leary's sister speaks:

X

My friend and my treasure!
There's many a handsome woman
From Cork of the sails
To the bridge of Toames
With a great herd of cattle

And gold for her dowry,
That would not have slept soundly
On the night we were waking you.

Eileen speaks:

XI

My friend and my lamb;
You must never believe it,
Nor the whisper that reached you,
Nor the venomous stories
That said I was sleeping.
It was not sleep was on me,
But your children were weeping,
And they needed me with them
To bring their sleep to them.

XII

Now judge, my people,
What woman in Ireland
That at every nightfall
Lay down beside him,
That bore his three children,
Would not lose her reason
After Art O'Leary
That's here with me vanquished
Since yesterday morning?

Arthur O'Leary's father speaks:

XIII

Bad luck to you, Morris! –
May your heart's blood poison you!
With your squint eyes gaping!
And your knock-knees breaking! –
That murdered my darling,
And no man in Ireland
To fill you with bullets.

XIV

My friend and my heart!
Rise up again now, Art,

Leap up on your horse,
Make straight for Macroom town,
Then to Inchigeela back,
A bottle of wine in your fist,
The same as you drank with your dad.

Eileen speaks:

XV

My bitter, long torment
That I was not with you
When the bullet came towards you,
My right side would have taken it
Or a fold of my tunic,
And I would have saved you
Oh smooth-handed rider.

Arthur O'Leary's sister speaks:

XVI

My sore sharp sorrow
That I was not behind you
When the gun-powder blazed at you,
My right side would have taken it,
Or a fold of my gown,
And you would have gone free then
Oh grey-eyed rider,
Since you were a match for them.

Eileen speaks:

XVII

My friend and my treasure!
It's bad treatment for a hero
To lie hooded in a coffin,
The warm-hearted rider
That fished in bright rivers,
That drank in great houses
With white-breasted women.
My thousand sorrows
That I've lost my companion.

XVIII

Bad luck and misfortune
Come down on you, Morris!
That snatched my protector,
My unborn child's father:
Two of them walking
And the third still within me,
And not likely I'll bear it.

XIX

My friend and my pleasure!
When you went out through the gateway
You turned and came back quickly,
You kissed your two children,
You kissed me on the forehead,
You said: 'Eileen, rise up quickly,
Put your affairs in order
With speed and with decision.
I am leaving home now
And there's no telling if I'll return.'
I mocked this way of talking,
He had said it to me so often.

XX

My friend and my dear!
Oh bright-sworded rider,
Rise up this moment,
Put on your fine suit
Of clean, noble cloth,
Put on your black beaver,
Pull on your gauntlets.
Up with your whip;
Outside your mare is waiting.
Take the narrow road east,
Where the trees thin before you,
Where streams narrow before you,
Where men and women will bow before you,
If they keep their old manners –
But I fear they have lost them.

XXI

My love and my treasure!
Not my dead ancestors,
Nor the deaths of my three children,
Nor Domhnall Mór O'Connell,
Nor Connall that drowned at sea,
Nor the twenty-six years woman
Who went across the water
And held kings in conversation –
It's not on all of them I'm calling
But on Art who was slain last night
At the inch of Carriganima! –
The brown mare's rider
That's here with me only –
With no living soul near him
But the dark little women of the mill,
And my thousand sorrows worsened
That their eyes were dry of tears.

XXII

My friend and my lamb!
Arthur O'Leary,
Of Connor, of Keady,
Of Louis O'Leary,
From west in Geeragh
And from east in Caolchnoc,
Where berries grow freely
And gold nuts on branches
And great floods of apples
All in their seasons.
Would it be a wonder
If Ive Leary were blazing
Besides Ballingeary
And Guagán of the saint
For the firm-handed rider
That hunted the stag down,
All out from Grenagh
When slim hounds fell behind?
And Oh clear-sighted rider,
What happened last night?
For I thought to myself
That nothing could kill you
Though I bought your habit.

Arthur O'Leary's sister speaks:

XXIII

My friend and my love!
Of the country's best blood,
That kept eighteen wet-nurses at work,
And each received her pay –
A heifer and a mare,
A sow and her litter,
A mill at the ford,
Yellow gold and white silver,
Silks and fine velvets,
A holding of land –
To give her milk freely
To the flower of fair manhood.

XXIV

My love and my treasure
And my love, my white dove!
Though I did not come to you,
Nor bring my troops with me,
That was no shame to me
For they were all enclosed
In shut-up rooms,
In narrow coffins,
In sleep without waking.

XXV

Were it not for the small-pox
And the black death
And the spotted fever,
That powerful army
Would be shaking their harness
And making a clatter
On their way to your funeral,
Oh white-breasted Art.

XXVI

My love you were and my joy!
Of the blood of those rough horsemen
That hunted in the valley,
Till you turned them homewards
And brought them to your hall,

Where knives were being sharpened,
Pork laid out for carving
And countless ribs of mutton,
The red-brown oats were flowing
To make the horses gallop –
Slender, powerful horses
And stable-boys to care them
Who would not think of sleeping
Nor of deserting their horses
If their owners stayed a week,
Oh brother of many friends.

XXVII

My friend and my lamb!
A cloudy vision
Came last night to me
In Cork at midnight
Alone in my bed:
That our white court fell,
That the Geeragh withered,
That your slim hounds were still
And the birds without sweetness
When you were found vanquished
On the side of the mountain,
Without priest or cleric
But an old shrivelled woman
That spread her cloak over you,
Arthur O'Leary,
While your blood flowed freely
On the breast of your shirt.

XXVIII

My love and my treasure!
And well they suited you,
Five-ply stockings,
Boots to your knees,
A three-cornered Caroline,
A lively whip,
On a frisky horse –
Many a modest, mannerly maiden
Would turn to gaze after you.

Eileen speaks:

XXIX

My love forever!
And when you went in cities,
Strong and powerful,
The wives of the merchants
All bowed down to you
For they knew in their hearts
What a fine man in bed you were,
And what a fine horseman
And father for children.

XXX

Jesus Christ knows
I'll have no cap on my head,
Nor a shift on my back,
Nor shoes on my feet,
Nor goods in my house,
Nor the brown mare's harness
That I won't spend on lawyers;
That I'll cross the seas
And talk to the king,
And if no one listens
That I'll come back
To the black-blooded down
That took my treasure from me.

XXXI

My love and my darling!
If my cry were heard westwards
To great Derrynane
And to gold-appled Capling,
Many swift, hearty riders
And white-kerchiefed women
Would be coming here quickly
To weep at your waking,
Beloved Art O'Leary.

XXXII

My heart is warming
To the fine women of the mill
For their goodness in lamenting
The brown mare's rider.

XXXIII

May your black heart fail you,
Oh false John Cooney!
If you wanted a bribe,
You should have asked me.
I'd have given you plenty:
A powerful horse
That would carry you safely
Through the mob
When the hunt is out for you,
Or a fine herd of cattle,
Or ewes to bear lambs for you,
Or the suit of a gentleman
With spurs and top-boots –
Though it's sorry I'd be
To see you done up in them,
For I've always heard
You're a piddling lout.

XXIV

Oh white-handed rider,
Since you are struck down,
Rise and go after Baldwin,
The ugly wretch
With the spindle shanks,
And take your revenge
For the loss of your mare –
May he never enjoy her.
May his six children wither!
But no bad wish to Máire
Though I have no love for her,
But that my own mother
Gave space in her womb to her
For three long seasons.

XXV

My love and my dear!
Your stooks are standing,
Your yellow cows milking;
On my heart is such sorrow
That all Munster could not cure it,
Nor the wisdom of the sages.

Till Art O'Leary returns
There will be no end to the grief
That presses down on my heart,
Closed up tight and firm
Like a trunk that is locked
And the key is mislaid.

XXXVI

All you women out there weeping,
Wait a little longer;
We'll drink to Art son of Connor
And the souls of all the dead,
Before he enters the school –
Not learning wisdom or music
But weighed down by earth and stones.

EIBHLÍN DHUBH NÍ CHONAILL (c.1743-c.1800)
translated from the Irish by Eilís Dillon

Remember

Remember me when I am gone away,
    Gone far away into the silent land;
    When you can no more hold me by the hand,
Nor I half turn to go yet turning stay.
Remember me when no more day by day
    You tell me of our future that you planned:
    Only remember me; you understand
It will be late to counsel then or pray.
Yet if you should forget me for a while
    And afterwards remember, do not grieve:
    For if the darkness and corruption leave
    A vestige of the thoughts that once I had,
Better by far you should forget and smile
    Than that you should remember and be sad.

CHRISTINA ROSSETTI (1830-94)

Dead Woman

If suddenly you do not exist,
if suddenly you no longer live,
I shall live on.

I do not dare,
I do not dare to write it,
if you die.

I shall live on.

For where a man has no voice,
there shall be my voice.

Where blacks are flogged and beaten,
I cannot be dead.
When my brothers go to prison
I shall go with them.

When victory,
not my victory,
but the great victory
comes,
even if I am dumb I must speak;
I shall see it coming even if I am blind.

No, forgive me.
If you no longer live,
if you, beloved, my love,
if you
have died,
all the leaves will fall on my breast,
it will rain on my soul night and day,
the snow will burn my heart,
I shall walk with frost and fire and death and snow,
my feet will want to walk to where you are sleeping,
but
I shall stay alive,
because above all things you wanted me

indomitable,
and, my love, because you know that I am not only a man
but all mankind.

PABLO NERUDA (1904-73)
translated from the Spanish by Brian Cole

Song for a Dark Girl

Way Down South in Dixie
    (Break the heart of me)
They hung my black young lover
    To a cross roads tree.

Way Down South in Dixie
    (Bruised body high in air)
I asked the white Lord Jesus
    What was the use of prayer.

Way Down South in Dixie
    (Break the heart of me)
Love is a naked shadow
    On a gnarled and naked tree.

LANGSTON HUGHES (1902-67)

Lost Love

His eyes are quickened so with grief,
He can watch a grass or leaf
Every instant grow; he can
Clearly through a flint wall see,
Or watch the startled spirit flee
From the throat of a dead man.
    Across two counties he can hear
And catch your words before you speak.
The woodlouse or the maggot's weak
Clamour rings in his sad ear,
And noise so slight it would surpass
Credence – drinking sound of grass,
Worm talk, clashing jaws of moth
Chumbling holes in cloth;
The groan of ants who undertake
Gigantic loads for honour's sake,
(Their sinews creak, their breath comes thin);
Whir of spiders when they spin,
And minute whispering, mumbling, sighs
Of idle grubs and flies.
    This man is quickened so with grief,
He wanders god-like or like thief
Inside and out, below, above,
Without relief seeking lost love.

ROBERT GRAVES (1895-1985)

Requiescat

Tread lightly, she is near
    Under the snow
Speak gently, she can hear
    The daisies grow.

All her bright golden hair
   Tarnished with rust,
She that was young and fair
   Fallen to dust.

Lily-like, white as snow,
   She hardly knew
She was a woman, so
   Sweetly she grew.

Coffin-board, heavy stone,
   Lie on her breast,
I vex my heart alone,
   She is at rest.

Peace, Peace, she cannot hear
   Lyre or sonnet,
All my life's buried here,
   Heap earth upon it.

OSCAR WILDE (1854-1900)

I want to talk to thee

I want to talk to thee of many things
Or sit in silence when the robin sings
His little song, when comes the winter bleak
I want to sit beside thee, cheek to cheek.

I want to hear thy voice my name repeat,
To fill my heart with echoes ever sweet;
I want to hear thy love come calling me
I want to seek and find but thee, but thee.

I want to talk to thee of little things
So fond, so frail, so foolish that one clings
To keep them ours – who could but understand
A joy in speaking them, thus hand in hand

Beside the fire; our joys, our hopes, our fears,
Our secret laughter, or unchidden tears;
Each day old dreams come back with beating wings,
I want to speak of these forgotten things.

I want to feel thy arms around me pressed,
To hide my weeping eyes upon thy breast;
I want thy strength to hold and comfort me
For all the grief I had in losing thee.

DORA SIGERSON (1866-1918)

The Apparition

My pillow won't tell me
    Where he has gone,
The soft-footed one
    Who passed by, alone.

Who took my heart, whole,
    With a tilt of his eye,
And with it, my soul,
    And it like to die.

I twist, and I turn,
    My breath but a sigh.
Dare I grieve? Dare I mourn?
    He walks by. He walks by.

THEODORE ROETHKE (1908-63)

Me, Me, and None But Me

Me, me, and none but me, dart home, O gently Death,
And quickly, for I draw too long this idle breath.
O how long till I may fly to Heaven above
Unto my faithful and beloved turtle dove.

Like to the silver swan, before my death I sing;
And, yet alive, my fatal knell I help to ring.
Still I desire from earth and earthly joys to fly.
He never happy lived that cannot love to die.

JOHN DOWLAND (1563-1626)

The Sunlight on the Garden

The sunlight on the garden
Hardens and grows cold,
We cannot cage the minute
Within its nets of gold,
When all is told
We cannot beg for pardon.

Our freedom as free lances
Advances towards its end;
The earth compels, upon it
Sonnets and birds descend;
And soon, my friend,
We shall have no time for dances.

The sky was good for flying
Defying the church bells
And every evil iron
Siren and what it tells:
The earth compels,
We are dying, Egypt, dying.

And not expecting pardon,
Hardened in heart anew,
But glad to have sat under
Thunder and rain with you,
And grateful too
For sunlight on the garden.

LOUIS MacNEICE (1907-63)

In Moonlight, Somewhere, They Are Singing
(from 'Some Quiet, Plain Poems')

Under the maples at moonrise –
Moon whitening top leaf of the white oak
That rose from the dark mass of maples and range of eyes –
They were singing together, and I woke

From my sleep to the whiteness of moon-fire,
And deep from their dark maples, I
Could hear the two voices shake silver and free, and aspire
To be lost in moon-vastness of the sky.

My young aunt and her young husband
From their dark maples sang, and though
Too young to know what it meant I was happy and
So slept, for I knew I would come to know.

But what of the old man awake there,
As the voices, like vine, climbed up moonlight?
What thought did he think of past time as they twined bright in
        moon-air
And veined, with their silver, the moon-flesh of night?

Far off, I recall, in the barn lot,
A mule stamped, once; but the song then
Was over, and for that night, or forever, would not
Resume – but should it again,

Now years later, wake me to white moon-fire
On pillow, high oak leaf, and far field,
I should hope to find imaged in whatever new voices aspire
Some faith in life yet, by my years, unrepealed.

ROBERT PENN WARREN (1905-89)

'Belovèd, my Belovèd'
(Sonnets from the Portuguese, XX)

Belovèd, my Belovèd, when I think
That thou wast in the world a year ago,
What time I sate alone here in the snow
And saw no footprint, heard the silence sink
No moment at thy voice, but, link by link,
When counting all my chains, as if that so
They never could fall off at any blow
Struck by thy possible hand,   why, thus I drink
Of life's great cup of wonder! Wonderful,
Never to feel thee thrill the day or night
With personal act or speech, – nor ever cull
Some prescience of thee with the blossoms white
Thou sawest growing! Atheists are as dull,
Who cannot guess God's presence out of sight.

ELIZABETH BARRETT BROWNING (1806-61)

Late Fragment

And did you get what
you wanted from this life, even so?
I did.
And what did you want?
To call myself beloved, to feel myself
beloved on the earth.

RAYMOND CARVER (1939-88)

An Arundel Tomb

Side by side, their faces blurred,
The earl and countess lie in stone,
Their proper habits vaguely shown
As jointed armour, stiffened pleat,
And that faint hint of the absurd –
The little dogs under their feet.

Such plainness of the pre-baroque
Hardly involves the eye, until
It meets his left-hand gauntlet, still
Clasped empty in the other; and
One sees, with a sharp tender shock,
His hand withdrawn, holding her hand.

They would not think to lie so long.
Such faithfulness in effigy
Was just a detail friends would see:
A sculptor's sweet commissioned grace
Thrown off in helping to prolong
The Latin names around the base.

They would not guess how early in
Their supine stationary voyage
The air would change to soundless damage,
Turn the old tenantry away;
How soon succeeding eyes begin
To look, not read. Rigidly they

Persisted, linked, through lengths and breadths
Of time. Snow fell, undated. Light
Each summer thronged the glass. A bright
Litter of birdcalls strewed the same
Bone-riddled ground. And up the paths
The endless altered people came,

Washing at their identity.
Now, helpless in the hollow of
An unarmorial age, a trough
Of smoke in slow suspended skeins
Above their scrap of history,
Only an attitude remains:

Time has transfigured them into
Untruth. The stone fidelity
They hardly meant has come to be
Their final blazon, and to prove
Our almost-instinct almost true:
What will survive of us is love.

PHILIP LARKIN (1922-85)

ACKNOWLEDGEMENTS

The poems in this anthology are either out of copyright or reprinted from the following books, all by permission of the publishers listed unless stated otherwise. Thanks are due to all the copyright holders cited below for their kind permission:

Fleur Adcock: *Poems 1960-2000* (Bloodaxe Books, 2000); **John Agard**: *From the Devil's Pulpit* (Bloodaxe Books, 1997); **Conrad Aiken**: *Collected Poems* (Oxford University Press, Inc., New York, 1953, 1970), by permission of Joseph I. Killorin; **Gillian Allnutt**: *Beginning the Avocado* (Virago Press, 1987), by permission of the author; **Yehuda Amichai**, by permission of the author's estate; **Simon Armitage**: *Zoom!* (Bloodaxe Books, 1989); **W.H. Auden**: *Collected Poems*, ed. Edward Mendelson (Faber & Faber, 1991).

Charles Baudelaire: *Complete Poems*, trs. Walter Martin (Carcanet Press, 1997); **James K. Baxter**: *Collected Poems* (Oxford University Press, NZ, 1979), by permission of Mrs J.C. Baxter; **Samuel Beckett**: *Collected Poems 1930-1979* (Calder Publications, 1984); **Marvin Bell**: *Nightworks: Poems 1962-2000* (Copper Canyon Press, 2000); **Hilaire Belloc**: *Complete Verse* (Duckworth, 1958), by permission of Peters, Fraser & Dunlop; **James Berry**: *Lucy's Letters and Loving* (New Beacon Books, 1982), by permission of the author; **John Berryman**: *His Toy, His Dream, His Rest* (Faber & Faber, 1969); **John Betjeman**: *Collected Poems* (John Murray, 1958); **Bhartrhari**: from John Brough (trs.), *Poems from the Sanskrit* (Penguin, 1968); **Sujata Bhatt**: *Point No Point* (Carcanet Press, 1997); **Elizabeth Bishop**: *The Complete Poems 1927-1979* (Chatto & Windus, 1983), by permission of Farrar, Straus & Giroux, Inc; **Edmund Blunden**: *An Elegy and Other Poems*, from *Collected Poems* (Duckworth, 1930), by permission of Peters, Fraser & Dunlop; **Kamau Brathwaite**: *Other Exiles* (Oxford University Press, 1975); **André Bréton**: 'Freedom of Love', trs. Edouard Roditi, reprinted by permission of the author's estate; **Eleanor Brown**: *Maiden Speech* (Bloodaxe Books, 1996); **Alan Brownjohn**: *Collected Poems 1952-1983* (Secker & Warburg, 1983), by permission of the author.

David Campbell: *Collected Poems* (Angus & Robertson Australia, 1989); **Raymond Carver**: *All of Us: Collected Poems* (Harvill Press, 1996), by permission of International Creative Management, Inc., copyright © 1996 Tess Gallagher; **Nina Cassian**: *Life Sentence: Selected Poems*, ed. William Jay Smith (Anvil Press Poetry, 1990); **Catullus**: trs. Josephine Balmer, from *Catullus: Poems of Love and Hate* (Bloodaxe Books, 2004); **Catullus**: see also Ezra Pound; **Kate Clanchy**: *Slattern* (Chatto & Windus, 1995; Picador, 2001), by permission of Macmillan Publishers Ltd; **Austin Clarke**: *Collected Poems* (Dolmen Press in association with Oxford University Press, 1974), by permission of R. Dardis Clarke, 21 Pleasants Street, Dublin 8; **Billy Collins**: *Taking Off Emily Dickinson's Clothes: Selected Poems* (Picador, 2000), by permission of Macmillan Publishers Ltd; **Padraic Colum**: *The Poet's Circuits* (Oxford University Press, 1960); **Tony Conran**: *Welsh Verse* (Poetry Wales Press, 1986), by permission of the author; **David Constantine**: *Selected Poems* (Bloodaxe Books, 1991); **Wendy Cope**: *Serious Concerns* (Faber & Faber, 1992); **Frances Cornford**: *Collected Poems* (Barrie & Jenkins, 1954), by permission of Barr Ellison Solicitors; **Noel Coward**: *Collected Verse*, ed. Graham Payne & Martin Tickner (Methuen, 1984); **Robert Crawford**: *A Scottish Assembly* (Jonathan Cape, 1990), by permission of the Random House Group; **Robert**

Creeley: *Poems 1950-1965* (Marion Boyars Publishers, 1966); **E.E. Cummings:** *Complete Poems 1904-1962* (Liveright, 1994), by permission of W.W. Norton & Company, copyright © 1991 by the Trustees for the E.E. Cummings Trust and George James Firmage.

Peter Dale: *Edge to Edge: Selected Poems* (Anvil Press Poetry, 1996), by permission of the author; **Jonathan Davidson:** *A Horse Called House* (Smith/ Doorstop Books, 1997); **Walter de la Mare:** *The Complete Poems of Walter de la Mare* (Faber & Faber, 1969), by permission of the Literary Trustees of Walter de la Mare and the Society of Authors; **Pierre de Ronsard:** from Alistair Elliot (trs.), *French Love Poems* (Bloodaxe Books, 1991); **Edwin Denby:** *Collected Poems* (Full Court Press, New York, 1975); **Emily Dickinson:** *The Poems of Emily Dickinson*, ed. Ralph W. Franklin (Harvard University Press, 1998); **Eibhlín Dhubh Ní Chonaill:** 'The Lament for Arthur O'Leary, trs. Eilís Dillon, *Irish University Review*, vol. 1 no.2 (1971), by permission of Eiléan Ní Chuilleanáin; **Michael Donaghy:** *Dances Learned Last Night: Poems 1975-1995* (Picador, 2000), by permission of Macmillan Publishers Ltd; **H.D.** (Hilda Doolittle): *Collected Poems* (Carcanet Press, 1984); **Mark Doty:** *Sweet Machine* (Jonathan Cape, 1998), by permission of the Random House Group; **Rita Dove:** *Selected Poems* (Pantheon Books, 1993) by permission of the author; **Freda Downie:** *Collected Poems*, ed. George Szirtes (Bloodaxe Books, 1995); **Carol Ann Duffy:** *Selling Manhattan* (Anvil Press Poetry, 1987), *Mean Time* (Anvil Press Poetry, 1993/1998), by permission of Anvil Press Poetry; *The World's Wife* (Picador, 1999), by permission of Macmillan Publishers Ltd; **Ian Duhig:** *The Bradford Count* (Bloodaxe Books, 1991), by permission of the author; **Helen Dunmore:** *Out of the Blue: Poems 1975-2001* (Bloodaxe Books, 2001); **Nessie Dunsmuir:** *Ten Poems* (The Greville Press, 1988); **Paul Durcan:** *The Berlin Wall Café* (Blackstaff Press, 1985; Harvill Press, 1995), by permission of the Random House Group; **Bob Dylan:** *Writings and Drawings* (Grafton Books, 1984), by permission of Special Rider Music.

U.A. Fanthorpe: *Safe as Houses* (Peterloo Poets, 1995); **Vicki Feaver:** *The Handless Maiden* (Jonathan Cape, 1994), by permission of the Random House Group Ltd; **James Fenton:** *Out of Danger* (Penguin, 1993), by permission of Peters, Fraser & Dunlop Ltd; **Linda France:** *Red* (Bloodaxe Books, 1992); **Robert Frost:** *The Poetry of Robert Frost*, ed. Edward Connery Lathem (Jonathan Cape, 1967), by permission of Random House Group Ltd.

Tess Gallagher: *Portable Kisses* (Bloodaxe Books, 1996); **Lorna Goodison:** *I Am Becoming My Mother* (New Beacon Books, 1986); **W.S. Graham:** *Collected Poems* (Faber & Faber, 1979), by permission of Michael & Margaret Snow; **Robert Graves:** *Complete Poems*, ed. Beryl Graves and Dunstan Ward (Carcanet Press, 1995-1999); **Lavinia Greenlaw:** *A World Where News Travelled Slowly* (Faber & Faber, 1997); **Thom Gunn:** *The Man with Night Sweats* (Faber & Faber, 1992).

Sophie Hannah: *The Hero and the Girl Next Door* (Carcanet Press, 1995) **Gwen Harwood:** *The Lion's Bride* (Angus & Robertson, 1981), by permission of John Harwood; **Anne Haverty:** *The Beauty of the Moon* (Chatto & Windus, 1999), by permission of the Random House Group; **Dermot Healy:** *The Bally-connell Colours* (Gallery Press, 1992); **Seamus Heaney:** *Opened Ground: Poems 1966-1996* (Faber & Faber, 1998); **Judith Herzberg:** from *Nine Dutch Poets* (Uitgeverij de Harmonie); **Rita Ann Higgins:** *Sunny Side Plucked: New & Selected Poems* (Bloodaxe Books, 1996); **Selima Hill:** *Trembling Hearts in the Bodies of Dogs: New & Selected Poems* (Bloodaxe Books, 1994); **Miroslav**

Holub: *Poems Before & After: Collected English Translations* (Bloodaxe Books, 1990); **A.D. Hope:** *Selected Poems* (Carcanet Press, 1986); **A.E. Housman:** *The Collected Poems* (Jonathan Cape, 1939), by permission of the Society of Authors as the literary representative of the Estate of A.E. Housman; **Langston Hughes:** *The Collected Poems of Langston Hughes* (Knopf, NY, 1994), by permission of David Higham Associates; **Ted Hughes:** poems from *New Selected Poems* (Faber & Faber, 1995), reprinted from his Faber collections *Crow* (1972) and *Season Songs* (1976).

    Nigel Jenkins: *Acts of Union: Selected Poems 1974-1989* (Gwasg Gomer, 1990), by permission of the author; **Elizabeth Jennings:** *New Collected Poems* (Carcanet Press, 2002), by permission of David Higham Associates; **Peter Jolliffe:** 'Lacuna' by permission of the author.

    Patrick Kavanagh: *Selected Poems*, ed. Antoinette Quinn (Penguin, 1996), reprinted here by permission of the Trustees of the Estate of the late Katherine B. Kavanagh, and through the Jonathan Williams Literary Agency; **Jackie Kay:** *Two's Company* (Puffin, 1992), *Other Lovers* (Bloodaxe Books, 1993); **Brendan Kennelly:** *Love of Ireland: poems from the Irish* (Mercier Press, 1989), by permission of the translator; **Thomas Kinsella:** 'The Lovely Étan' from *The New Oxford Book of Irish Verse*, ed. & trs Thomas Kinsella (Oxford University Press, 1989), by permission of Carcanet Press Ltd.

    Philip Larkin: *The Less Deceived* (The Marvell Press, 1955), by permission of the Marvell Press, England and Australia; *The Whitsun Weddings* (Faber & Faber, 1964), reprinted in *Collected Poems*, ed. Anthony Thwaite (Faber & Faber, 1990); **Michael Laskey:** *The Tightrope Wedding* (Smith/Doorstop Books, 1999), by permission of the author; **D.H. Lawrence:** *Complete Poems* (Penguin, 1977), by permission of Laurence Pollinger Ltd; **Shane Leslie:** *Rhyme Street* (The Poetry Bookshop), by permission of the Estate of Sir Shane Leslie; **Primo Levi:** *Collected Poems*, trs. Ruth Feldman & Brian Swann (Faber & Faber, 1988); **Liz Lochhead:** *True Confessions and New Clichés* (Polygon, 1985); **Christopher Logue:** *Selected Poems* (Faber & Faber, 1996); **Michael Longley:** *Selected Poems* (Jonathan Cape, 1998), by permission of Lucas Alexander Whitley; **Federico García Lorca:** *Selected Poems*, trs. Merryn Williams (Bloodaxe Books, 1992); **Robert Lowell:** *For Lizzie & Harriet* (Faber & Faber, 1973); **Thomas Lynch:** *Skating with Heather Grace* (Knopf, NY, 1986).

    James McAuley: *Collected Poems* (Angus & Robertson, Australia, 1980), by permission of HarperCollins Publishers, Australia; **Roger McGough:** *Blazing Fruit: Selected Poems 1967-1987* (Penguin, 1990), by permission of Peters, Fraser & Dunlop; **Louis MacNeice:** *Collected Poems*, ed. E.R. Dodds (Faber, 1979), by permission of David Higham Associates Ltd; **Sarah Maguire:** *Spilt Milk* (Secker & Warburg, 1991) by permission of the author; **Leo Marks:** *Between Silk and Cyanide* (HarperCollins, 1988), permission given by the late author © 1956; **Marichiko:** see Kenneth Rexroth; **Edna St Vincent Millay:** *Selected Poems* (Carcanet Press, 1992); **Adrian Mitchell:** *Greatest Hits: His 40 Golden Greats* (Bloodaxe Books, 1991), *Heart on the Left: Poems 1953-1984* (Bloodaxe Books, 1997), by permission of Peters, Fraser & Dunlop, with an educational health warning: Adrian Mitchell asks that none of his poems be used in connection with any examination whatsoever; **Naomi Mitchison:** *The Laburnum Branch* (Jonathan Cape, 1926), by permission of the Literary Estate of Naomi Mitchison; **Xu Zhi Mo:** 'Don't Pinch Me, Hurts', trs. Carolyn Choa, by permission of Judy Daish Associates; **John Montague:** *Collected Poems* (Gallery Press, 1995); **Pete Morgan:** *The Spring Collection*

(Secker & Warburg, 1979), by permission of the author; **Andrew Motion:** *Selected Poems 1976-1997* (Faber & Faber, 1998); **Paul Muldoon:** *Hay* (Faber & Faber, 1997).

Pablo Neruda: *The Captain's Verses*, trs. Brian Cole (Anvil Press Poetry, 1994); **Grace Nichols:** *Lazy Thoughts of a Lazy Woman* (Virago Press, 1989), by permission of Curtis Brown Ltd.

Frank O'Connor: 'A Learned Mistress' by Isobel Campbell, from *Kings, Lords & Commons: Irish poems from the 7th century to the 19th century*, trs. Frank O'Connor (Gill & Macmillan, 1991), by permission of Peters, Fraser & Dunlop; **Frank O'Hara:** *Selected Poems* (Carcanet Press, 1991); **Sharon Olds:** *The Wellspring* (Jonathan Cape, 1996), by permission of the Random House Group Ltd; **Michael Ondaatje:** *The Cinnamon Peeler: Selected Poems* (Picador, 1989), by permission of the Ellen Levine Literary Agency, Inc; **Oodgeroo of the tribe Noonuccal:** *My People* (Jacaranda Press, 1990), by permission of John Wiley & Sons Australia; **Alice Oswald:** *The Thing in the Gap-Stone Stile* (Oxford University Press, 1996), by permission of Peters, Fraser & Dunlop.

Ruth Padel: *Rembrandt Would Have Loved You* (Chatto & Windus, 1998) by permission of the Random House Group; **Dorothy Parker:** *The Collected Dorothy Parker* (Penguin, 2001); **Brian Patten:** *Love Poems* (Flamingo Books, 1992); **Fernando Pessoa:** 'The Leaves' Audible Smile', trs. Paul Hyland, by permission of the translator; **Cole Porter:** *The Complete Lyrics of Cole Porter* (Hamish Hamilton, 1983); **Ezra Pound:** Catullus from *The Translations of Ezra Pound* (Faber & Faber, 1953); Ribaku from *Collected Shorter Poems* (Faber & Faber, 1926).

Deborah Randall: *The Sin Eater* (Bloodaxe Books, 1989); **Deryn Rees-Jones:** *Signs Round a Dead Body* (Seren Books, 1998); **Christopher Reid:** *Pea Soup* (Oxford University Press, 1982), by permission of the author; **Kenneth Rexroth:** *The Love Poems of Marichiko* (Christopher's Books, 1978); Petronius, from *Poems from the Greek Anthology* (University of Michigan Press, 1962); **Adrienne Rich:** *The Fact of a Doorframe: Poems Selected and New, 1950-1984* (W.W. Norton & Company, 1984), by permission of the author and W.W. Norton & Company; **Rainer Maria Rilke:** *Ahead of All Parting: The Selected Poetry and Prose of Rainer Maria Rilke*, tr. Stephen Mitchell (Picador, 1995), by permission of Macmillan Publishers Ltd; **Rainer Maria Rilke:** *Neue Geidichte / New Poems*, tr. Stephen Cohn (Carcanet Press, 1992); **Maurice Riordan:** *A Word from the Loki* (Faber & Faber, 1995); **Robin Robertson:** *A Painted Field* (Picador, 1997), by permission of Macmillan Publishers Ltd; **Theodore Roethke:** *Collected Poems* (Faber & Faber, 1968); **Tracy Ryan:** *The Willing Eye* (Bloodaxe Books/FACP, 1999).

Sonia Sanchez: *Homegirls & Handgrenades* (Thunder's Mouth Press, NY, 1984), reprinted in *Singing Coming Off the Drums: Love Poems* (Beacon Press, USA, 1999); **Peter Sansom:** *Everything You've Heard Is True* (Carcanet Press, 1990); **Sappho:** *Poems & Fragments*, trs. Josephine Balmer (Bloodaxe Books, 1992); **Gjertrud Schnackenberg:** *Supernatural Love: Poems 1976-2000* (Bloodaxe Books, 2001); **Solveig von Schoultz:** 'Conversation', from *Ice Around Our Lips: Finland-Swedish Poetry*, trs. David McDuff (Bloodaxe Books, 1989), by permission of the translator; **Delmore Schwartz:** *What Is To Be Given: Selected Poems* (New Directions, Inc., USA; Carcanet Press, 1976), by permission of Laurence Pollinger Ltd; **Vikram Seth:** *All You Who Sleep Tonight* (Faber & Faber, 1996); **Anne Sexton:** *Complete Poems*, ed. Maxine Kumin (Mariner Books, USA, 1999), by permission of Sterling Lord Literistic, Inc;

299

Jo Shapcott: *Her Book: Poems 1988-1998* (Faber & Faber, 2000); **Penelope Shuttle**: *Selected Poems* (Oxford University Press, 1997), by permission of David Higham Associates; **Elizabeth Smart**: *By Grand Central Station I Sat Down and Wept* (Editions Poetry London, 1945; Panther Books, 1966), by permission of Sebastian Barker; **Dave Smith**: *Homage to Edgar Allan Poe* (Louisiana State University Press, 1981), by permission of the author; **Stevie Smith**: *Collected Poems*, ed. James MacGibbon (Penguin, 1985), by permission of the James MacGibbon Estate; **Edith Södergran**: *Complete Poems*, trs. David McDuff (Bloodaxe Books, 1984); **William Stafford**: *The Darkness Around Us Is Deep* (HarperCollins, 1993); **Francis Stuart**: from *Irish Love Poems*, ed. Norman Jeffares (The O'Brien Press, 1997), by permission of the Estate of Francis Stuart; **Alicia Stubbersfield**: *Unsuitable Shoes* (The Collective Press, 1999); **Wislawa Szymborska**: *View with a Grain of Sand: Selected Poems*, trs. Stanislaw Baranczak & Clare Cavanagh (Harcourt Brace & Company, 1993).

Victor Tapner: 'Coffee Shop' from *The Dulwich Poetry Festival Competition Anthology* (Dulwich Poetry Festival, 1998), by permission of the author; **R.S. Thomas**: 'Madrigal' from *The Stones of the Field* (Druid Press, Carmarthen, 1946), by permission of the Estate of R.S. Thomas; **Henry Treece**: *Collected Poems* (Knopf, NY, 1946), by permission of the John Johnson Agency; **Marina Tsvetayeva**: *Selected Poems*, trs. David McDuff (Bloodaxe Books, 1987).

John Wain: *Poems 1949-1979* (Macmillan, 1980), by permission of Curtis Brown Ltd on behalf of the Estate of John Wain; **Arthur Waley**: *170 Chinese Poems* (Constable Publishers, 1918); **Chris Wallace-Crabbe**: *Selected Poems 1956-1994* (Oxford University Press, 1995), by permission of Carcanet Press; **Robert Penn Warren**: *You, Emperors and Others* (1960), reprinted in *Selected Poems* (Random House, 1966); **E.B.White**: *Poems and Sketches of E.B. White* (Harper & Row, 1981), by permission of the Estate of E.B. White; **Richard Wilbur**: *New and Collected Poems* (Harcourt Brace Jovanovich, USA, 1988; Faber & Faber, 1989); **C.K. Williams**: *New & Selected Poems* (Farrar, Straus & Giroux, Inc., USA; Bloodaxe Books, 1995); **Hugo Williams**: *Collected Poems* (Faber & Faber, 2002); **Sheila Wingfield**: *Collected Poems 1938-1983* (Enitharmon Press, 1983); **James Wright**: *Above the River: Complete Poems* (Farrar, Straus & Giroux, Inc., USA, 1990; Bloodaxe Books, 1992), by permission of Wesleyan University Press; **Judith Wright**: *Collected Poems* (Carcanet Press, 1992); **Kit Wright**: *Hoping It Might Be So: Poems 1974-2000* (Leviathan, 2000), by permission of Michael Hulse.

W.B. Yeats: *The Poems*, ed. Richard J. Finneran (Macmillan, 1991), by permission of A.P. Watt Ltd on behalf of Michael B. Yeats.

Every effort has been made to trace copyright holders of the poems published in this book. The editor and publisher apologise if any material has been included without permission or without the appropriate acknowledgement, and would be glad to be told of anyone who has not been consulted.

INDEX OF AUTHORS & TRANSLATORS

INDEX OF TITLES & FIRST LINES

308

311

Staying Alive
real poems for unreal times
edited by NEIL ASTLEY

Staying Alive is an international anthology of 500 life-affirming poems fired by belief in the human and the spiritual at a time when much in the world feels unreal, inhuman and hollow. These are poems of great personal force connecting our aspirations with our humanity, helping us stay alive to the world and stay true to ourselves.

'*Staying Alive* is a blessing of a book. The title says it all. I have long waited for just this kind of setting down of poems. Has there ever been such a passionate anthology? These are poems that hunt you down with the solace of their recognition' – ANNE MICHAELS.

'*Staying Alive* is a book which leaves those who have read or heard a poem from it feeling less alone and more alive' – JOHN BERGER.

'*Staying Alive* is a magnificent anthology. The last time I was so excited, engaged and enthralled by a collection of poems was when I first encountered *The Rattle Bag*' – PHILIP PULLMAN

'A vibrant, brilliantly diverse anthology of poems to delight the mind, heart and soul. A book for people who know they love poetry, and for people who think they don't' – HELEN DUNMORE.

'*Staying Alive* is a wonderful testament to Neil Astley's lifetime in poetry, and to the range and courage of his taste. It's also, of course, a testament to poetry itself: to its powers to engross and move us, to its ability to challenge and brace us, and to its exultation. Everyone who cares about poetry should own this book' – ANDREW MOTION.

'This is a book to make you fall in love with poetry...Go out and buy it for everyone you love' – CHRISTINA PATTERSON, *Independent*

'Anyone who has the faintest glimmer of interest in modern poetry must buy it. If I were master of the universe or held the lottery's purse strings, there would be a copy of it in every school, public library and hotel bedroom in the land...I found myself laughing, crying, wondering, rejoicing, reliving, wishing, envying. It is a book full of hope and high art which restores your faith in poetry' – ALAN TAYLOR, *Sunday Herald*

'These poems, just words, distil the human heart as nothing else' – JANE CAMPION.

Pleased to See Me

69 very sexy poems

edited by NEIL ASTLEY

'Is that a gun in your pocket, or are you just pleased to see me?'
— MAE WEST

Mae West's racy wisecrack could have been aimed at this book, which is packed with 69 high-calibre, sharp-shooting poems. *Pleased to See Me* bulges with boldly playful and seriously sensual treatments of everything you ever wanted to know about sex...but never thought to find in a poem.

Editor Neil Astley caught the *zeitgeist* in *Staying Alive*. Now he turns to more intimate matters, bringing you a spicy selection of X-rated contemporary poems for reading in bed. *Pleased to See Me* covers and uncovers everything we like doing with our bodies...women and men. These are poems to have fun with. Read them to your lover. Make this your personal pillow book.

Pleased to See Me is a sassy and unashamedly saucy celebration of fleshly pleasures by some of our finest poets. 'These are very sexy poems not just because they are about sex,' says Astley, 'but because their luscious language is handled with wit and sureness of touch. This is the first book to show how the way poets write about sex has changed dramatically. As in so much else, the boundaries have shifted. Sex in modern poetry – as in films, novels and music – is treated freely and frankly, with passion, tenderness and a great sense of fun. Expect surprises and reversals as well as creepiness and unease, coupled with in-your-face exuberance. We're talking strong language and strong emotion here.'

The Book of Orgasms
NIN ANDREWS

'Borgesian fictions, Swiftian sex...sheer euphoria, sheer poetry'
– RACHEL JANE WEISS

An underground cult classic in the States, Nin Andrews' *Book of Orgasms* is a collection of playful fictions or prose poems, part human, part divine, leaping from our everyday world to explore the limits of bliss. She maps the imaginary terrain of that upper realm, the place where euphoria endures.

Nin Andrews' orgasms are those peak moments taking the form of invisible creatures that wait to lift us up into the air, out of the ordinary and into a place just above our heads, just beyond our fingertips. And yet – curse or blessing – the gravity of our own desire, the weight of our humanness, continually pulls us back from the splendid lightness of euphoria.

'There is no other young writer – at least not on these shores – whose work even remotely resembles that of Nin Andrews. To find her predecessors one has to look to Europe, to the sly and sometimes erotic zaniness of Luis Buñuel. Nin Andrews' *Book of Orgasms* is hilariously Swiftian and eerily surrealist by turns. Talents as original as hers are rare – and are exceedingly welcome' – DAVID WOJAHN.

'What a swell first book this is – sexy, audacious, funny, inventive. Nin Andrews has a deft comic touch that enhances her lyricism. Her commitment to pleasure is a salutary reminder that amusement contains muse. Read this book in bed. I'm sure it will be as good for you as it was for me' – DAVID LEHMAN.

French Love Poems

translated by **ALISTAIR ELLIOT**

POETRY BOOK SOCIETY RECOMMENDED TRANSLATION

French Love Poems is about the kinds of love that puzzle, delight and afflict us throughout our lives, from going on walks with an attractive cousin before Sunday dinner (Nerval) to indulging a grand-daughter (Hugo). On the way there's the first yes from lips we love (Verlaine), a sky full of stars reflected fatally in Cleopatra's eyes (Heredia), lying awake waiting for your lover (Valéry), and the defeated toys of dead children (Gautier).

The selection covers five centuries, from Ronsard to Valéry. Other poets represented include Baudelaire, Mallarmé, Rimbaud, La Fontaine, Laforgue and Leconte de Lisle. The 35 poems, chosen by Alistair Elliot, are printed opposite his own highly skilful verse translations. There are also helpful notes on French verse technique and on points of obscurity.

'Elliot is both a passionate and accurate translator and his Ronsard and Victor Hugo are as luminous as his versions of Verlaine and – that trap for most English translators – Mallarmé. Elliot is learned in Latin and Greek literature and this, combined with his natural lyricism and acute sense of form, make his French translations a scintillating collection' – ELIZABETH JENNINGS, *Sunday Telegraph*.

ALSO AVAILABLE FROM BLOODAXE:

Making for Planet Alice
New Women Poets
edited by MAURA DOOLEY

Why do we need another anthology of poetry solely by women? Several different groups of women writers emerged over the past thirty years who pioneered, fought to be published, reflected on subject-matter previously thought 'inappropriate' and who blazed into our consciousness with a train of glorious transgressions.

Now here is a group of new writers from Britain and Ireland who've absorbed and developed the recent legacies of other women poets. All thirty published their first collections during the past ten years. These are poets of the moment, writing with an energy, inventiveness and intelligence fit for the 21st century. They pay no attention to the restrictions of this universe. They're *Making for Planet Alice*. Prepare to be transported.

'An intelligent and often surprising appraisal of poetry by women... Their subjects and concerns are at once universal and particular, encompassing travel, science, ghosts, slugs, race and, of course, sex. The barbed debate of gender politics is ever present...Men be warned: you don't get off lightly here' – MAGGIE O'FARRELL, *Independent on Sunday*.

Including poems by: Moniza Alvi, Eleanor Brown, Siobhán Campbell, Kate Clanchy, Tessa Rose Chester, Julia Copus, Jane Duran, Gillian Ferguson, Janet Fisher, Linda France, Elizabeth Garrett, Lavinia Greenlaw, Vona Groarke, Sophie Hannah, Maggie Hannan, Tracey Herd, Jane Holland, Jackie Kay, Mimi Khalvati, Gwyneth Lewis, Sarah Maguire, Sinéad Morrissey, Ruth Padel, Katherine Pierpoint, Alice Oswald, Deryn Rees-Jones, Anne Rouse, Eva Salzman, Ann Sansom, Susan Wicks.